HOW TO USE YOUR HEALING POWER

A combined edition of Dr. Joseph Murphy's best-written works on healing:

How to Use Your Healing Power

The Miraculous Law of Healing

The Healing Power of Love

The Healing Power of Your Subconscious Mind

Meditations and Affirmations

DR. JOSEPH MURPHY

FiNGERPRINT!

Published 2019 by **FiNGER**PRINT!

An imprint of Prakash Books India Pvt. Ltd.

113/A, Darya Ganj, New Delhi-110 002,

Tel: (011) 2324 7062 – 65, Fax: (011) 2324 6975

Email: info@prakashbooks.com/sales@prakashbooks.com

facebook www.facebook.com/fingerprintpublishing

twitter www.twitter.com/FingerprintP

www.fingerprintpublishing.com

© JMW Group, Inc.

jmwgroup@jmwgroup.net

jmwforlife.com

Rights licensed exclusively by JMW Group Inc.

The author of this book does not dispense medical advice or prescribe the use of any technique as a form of treatment for physical, emotional, or medical problems without the advice of a physician, either directly or indirectly. The intent of the author is only to offer information of a general nature to help you in your quest for emotional and spiritual well-being. In the event you use any of the information in this book for yourself, which is your constitutional right, the author and the publisher assume no responsibility for your actions.

ISBN: 978 93 8905 377 7

Processed & printed in India

CONTENTS

HOW TO USE
YOUR HEALING POWER

INTRODUCTION

This book is written in response to thousands of requests from students in many parts of the world. One of the largest classes I have ever given was at the Wilshire Ebell Theatre, Los Angeles, California, on the healing miracles of Jesus and what they mean to men everywhere. This book is an attempt to elaborate on the inner meaning of the recorded healings in the New Testament and to show the reader that he can apply the Healing Principle today in the same way that Jesus did about two thousand years ago.

The stories of mental and physical illnesses recorded in the Bible have reoccurred from time immemorial to the present moment. You may see the conditions and symptoms of diseases described in the Bible in almost any hospital in the country. It is true, of course, that the diseases described today have scientific names derived from medical terminology.

All over the world today men and women of various creeds are awakening to the tremendous therapeutic results following the application of mental and spiritual laws. In the fields of medicine, psychiatry, psychology, and other related fields, evidence is being adduced and articles written on the effect of destructive mental and emotional conflicts as the cause of all kinds of disease. This is prophetic of the termination of the power of the five senses, the reign of so-called *matter*, and the reestablishment of the reign of Divine Intelligence and of the Infinite Healing Presence behind all things.

The Bible is a psychological textbook which teaches us how to overcome all problems. It explains how we get into trouble; then teaches us how to get out of trouble. It teaches a science of life. A knowledge of the meaning of symbols, the science of the Hebrew alphabet, and the meaning of the various names in the Bible forms the key to all the stories in the Bible. You may find the meaning of the various names given in the Bible in *Strong's Concordance* or *Young's Concordance*. There are many other reference books but the above two are generally used by all Bible students interested in the inner meaning of the Bible.

To fully understand what another speaks or writes, it is necessary to tune in with the writer, claiming and knowing that his ideas, thoughts, words, and feelings are reproduced in our mind. We do not really know who wrote the Gospels, and as I write or speak on these wonderful Bible stories, I say to my Deep Self in meditation, "What did I as the writer of these stories mean when I wrote them?" Then I get quiet and still, feeling the Living Intelligence within flowing through my conscious mind revealing to me everything I need to know. There is only one mind. A memory of everything that has ever transpired is within your subjective mind, and it is possible for you to tune in. In a state of intercommunion of mind with mind, it is possible to have transmitted to your mind all the thoughts, ideas, and feelings of another mind with which you are in tune or *en rapport*. This is possible without the ordinary channels of sensuous communication. There is but one mind common to all individual men.

The purpose of this book, so far as possible, is to divest and strip these stories of the Bible of all mystery so that it will be an open book for all mankind. The same Healing Presence which Moses, Elijah, Paul, and Jesus used is available to you now. Use it and go forward in the Light, moving from glory to glory *until the dawn appears, and the shadows flee away*.

Chapter

1

HEALING OF MENTAL DISORDERS

The following quotation is taken from the fourth chapter of Luke. It forms the sound basis for all healing, and tells all of us what we are here for.

The Spirit of the Lord is upon me, because he hath anointed me to preach the gospel to the poor; he hath sent me to heal the broken-hearted, to preach deliverance to the captives, and recovering of sight to the blind, to set at liberty them that are bruised. And he closed the book, and he gave it again to the minister, and sat down. And the eyes of all them that were in the synagogue were fastened on him. And he began to say unto them, This day is this scripture fulfilled in your ears. Luke 4:18-21.

Here is one of the most remarkable and extraordinary statements in the whole Bible. *This day is this scripture fulfilled* in your ears. Not tomorrow or next week or next year, but NOW, this minute. *God is the Eternal Now.* Your good is this moment. Claim your health now, your peace now. The Healing Principle and the Peace of God are within you. Someone asked me in our class on "The Healing Miracles" if the healing stories in the Bible were true. The answer to the question is very simple. If the use of the Healing Principle is going on all the time and is applicable to all people all of the time everywhere, it is certainly truer, more interesting, and more fascinating than if it were an historic event of a certain date, a definite geographical location, and confined to just certain people.

In order to understand your Bible see it as a great psychological drama taking place in the consciousness of all people everywhere when they pray scientifically. Look upon the following dramatic episodes recorded in the Bible as stories about yourself and your friends awakening from darkness to the Light within. You can call Jesus in the Bible, as Robert Taylor of Cambridge, England, in 1829 did, *illumined reason.* Your concordance gives you many meanings for Jesus such as "God is savior," or "God is your solution, or salvation." In other words the names Joshua and Jesus are identical. The meaning is that your awareness or faith in the God-Wisdom can do all things. Look upon Jesus as yourself possessed of faith and confidence looking at the thoughts, beliefs, and opinions of your mind (your synagogue) rejecting all the false beliefs, theories, and ideas and announcing the presence of your ideal or the state desired. You do this in the present tense.

The Bible writer tells you that no matter what you are seeking, it exists now. Why wait for a healing? Why postpone it? Why say, "Some day I will have peace." The God of peace is within. The Power of the Almighty is within, and you will receive energy and strength. Love is here this moment, and you can experience the Divine Love welling up in your heart for all people. You can also attract your divine companion now. What you are seeking in the future is present now, right where you are. Your knowledge of the laws of your mind is your savior.

And they were astonished at his doctrine: for his word was with power. And in the synagogue there was a man, which had a spirit of an unclean devil, and cried out with a loud voice, saying, Let us alone; what have we to do with thee, thou Jesus of Nazareth? Art thou come to destroy us? I know thee who thou art; the Holy One of God. And Jesus rebuked him, saying, Hold thy peace, and come out of him. And when the devil had thrown him in the midst, he came out of him, and hurt him not. Luke 4:32-35. *Related passages,* Mark 1:23-27, 3:11, 7:25-30.

There was a belief in ancient times that when a man was insane he was possessed by demons or devils. This had its corollary in the belief that all psychotic or mentally deranged people were demon possessed. In Bible days, exorcism in its varied forms became the regularly accepted form of therapy for the mentally disordered patients. Even today in some parts of America and even here in Los Angeles a student will say, "Oh, I think he or she is possessed by a demon." At one time people tried varying methods in order to drive demons out of the mind or body of the person. Today the psychiatrist, psychologist, and spiritual leader tries to bring about an adjustment of the personality and a cleansing of the mind of all negative thoughts and false beliefs. You are very familiar with the sudden and miraculous change often seen nowadays when a manic-depressive condition of an individual is cured by shock therapy.

Many years ago when a boy traveling on an ocean liner to India, I saw a raving maniac completely healed by an American woman who prayed aloud for him. He had a remarkable, instantaneous healing. Being curious, I asked her what she did. She replied, "I claimed that God's love and peace filled his mind." Today I understand much better what she meant. Her realization of the presence and power of God in the man was instantaneously resurrected in his mind, and a healing followed. Her faith made him whole. This is the whole story from a spiritual standpoint.

All *demons or devils* are negative states of mind that have been developed because the creative power of man has been used in an ignorant and destructive manner. The work of every man is to go into his own *synagogue* (mind) and through spiritual awareness cast out of his own mind the false theories, dogmas, beliefs, opinions, as well as all negative states such as resentment, ill will, hatred, jealousy, etc. These are the devils which bedevil us. Obsessions, dual personalities, and all other mental aberrations are the result of habitual negative thinking, crystallizing into definite states of mind such as complexes and other various poison pockets in the subconscious.

You are empowered to cast out demons by affirming your unity and oneness with the indwelling God; then you silently or audibly with feeling and faith speak the word of health, harmony,

11

and peace. Pray with confidence like the woman on board the ship referred to previously by silently concentrating on the dissolving Power of God's Love upon the person. Thus the hold of evil thoughts will be broken.

The supposed devil cries out, *Let us alone, what have we to do with thee. And he rebuked him saying, Hold thy peace, come out of him.*

To rebuke means that you completely reject, once and for all, the power of any so-called negative or evil force. You do not admit for one moment that demons have any power, or that there are such entities.

He suffered not the demons to speak. Mark 1:34.

This means that you, who are illumined by the Light, will not, under any circumstances, permit negative race thoughts to dissuade you to turn away from the belief in One Supreme Power which is One and Indivisible. The method of healing used by Jesus here was the word of authority . . . *for with authority and power he commandeth the unclean spirits, and they came out.* Luke 4:36.

Your word is your awareness, your feeling, your conviction. Psychologically it is the union of the conscious and subconscious mind; i.e., you have reached the point of agreement or complete mental acceptance of that which you affirm as true. The moment you accept it completely without reservations, the healing takes place in the person for whom you are praying. If you are praying for a mentally deranged person, follow the teachings of the Bible herein set forth.

Go boldly into your synagogue, which means the temple of your own mind; there gather your thoughts together rehearsing in your mind the Truths about God in the presence of your assembled thoughts and opinions; and therein feel the mental atmosphere of freedom and peace of mind for the sick person. Become Jesus (illumined mind) now; i.e., you are full of faith and confidence as you enter the realm of your mind, giving no power to symptoms, or the nature of the mental blocks. Reject completely the verdict and opinions of those around you. Do this emphatically and with a sense of inner knowing. Know that you have the authority to speak the word; i.e., to feel and know that your thought is authoritative inasmuch as it is the Infinite thinking through you.

Quimby, the great American healer, knew that when he thought of his patient he was in command of the other person's mind and body; then he contemplated his divine perfection. He duplicated many of the miracles recorded in the Bible. Quimby's inner conviction that what was true of God was true of his patient was the *word* that he sent. *He sent his word and healed them.*

There are many evil spirits (negative emotions) such as hatred, resentment, revenge, jealousy, etc. It could be said that a man with intense hatred is obsessed by an evil spirit. Your mood or emotion is the spirit operating at the human level. The law governing your subjective mind is that it is amenable to suggestion. In ancient times, the idea was current that any one was liable at any time to be taken possession of by a devil. Many persons who easily entered the subjective condition through fear found themselves possessed by devils, i.e., the power of their own fearful thoughts.

In ancient times and even today in some parts of the world the profession of exorcism was and is a very profitable one. The general belief was that the demons were afraid of holy water, the Bible, and of hearing the name of God pronounced. Accordingly it came to pass that, upon the verbal command of the exorcist the so-called devil would often incontinently fly, leaving the patient free. Sometimes the patient would go into convulsions on hearing the magic name pronounced, and more exorcists were then employed. You can see that the whole procedure is one of belief, and according to the belief of the exorcist is it done unto him.

Doctors and scientists are conducting experiments in hypnosis; they know, for example, that they can cause a subject under hypnosis to act like an insane person by suggestion. For instance, in a trance state a man can be told he will jump with one foot in the air when he sees a dog, and he will jump. If given a post-hypnotic suggestion, he will repeat the performance after being awakened. This is a compulsion. He can be told he is possessed by a bad spirit or devil, and his subconscious mind which acts upon suggestion, faithfully reproduces the role of a devil with the same extraordinary acumen that it would personate any other character suggested. The subconscious mind which is all things to all men will exhibit as many different kinds and degrees of deviltry as there are devils embraced in the suggestion. Experimentally any type of insanity can be brought about by appropriate suggestions given to subjects in the trance state. In experiments when the suggestion is relieved, the subject being instructed that it was only a suggestion, the mental aberrations disappear. The schizophrenic, psychotic, depressive type, manic type of insanities can be demonstrated by suggestion. It is easy to see where the so-called devils come from.

The ceremony of exorcism which is even today in use by certain organizations constitutes a most powerful suggestive command to the subjective mind; according to the faith of the operator the desired result is achieved. The fact that the trouble is susceptible of cure by a ritual or ceremony points clearly to its mental origin, precluding the possibility of its being attributable to extramundane causes or external entities.

Many people come to see me and write me saying that they hear voices all the time, and what terrible things these voices are saying. They believe they are possessed by evil spirits. I tell them that I hear voices also. Clairaudience is a faculty of the human mind. It is that faculty of intelligence within you which enables your objective mind to receive communications from your own subjective mind, or from another by means of spoken words.

A few weeks ago I clearly heard an answer to a question which had perplexed me for some time. I heard the words clearly. These words did not come from some discarnate entity but they came from my own subjective self which is one with Boundless Wisdom and Infinite Intelligence. When you receive ideas from the subjective, or when the answer comes, it is necessarily by such means as can be understood by you, i.e., by means which appeal to your senses. There are many people who hear clairaudiently; some attribute it to imagination, others regard it as a subjective hallucination. Some attribute this phenomenon of hearing words from the subjective mind to spirits of the departed; needless to say, the same law of suggestion applies and governs the character of their clairaudient manifestation.

The subconscious mind will assume the characters suggested by the conscious mind. If, for example, you believe it is a guardian angel speaking to you, or the voice of a disembodied spirit, the subconscious will follow the suggestion given, and all further communication will be conducted on the basis assumed by you. Your subconscious will assume the character of an angel or devil according to the suggestion given.

Some months ago a young man from a local university came to see me with the complaint that he was constantly hearing spirit-voices, that they made him do nasty things, and that they would not let him alone, neither would they permit him to read the Bible or other spiritual books. He was convinced that he was talking to supernatural beings. This young man was clairaudient, and not knowing that all people possess this faculty, he began to think it was due to evil spirits. His superstitious beliefs caused him to ascribe it to departed spirits. Through constant worry he became a monomaniac on the subject. His subconscious mind dominated and controlled by an all-potent but false suggestion, gradually took over control and mastery of his objective faculties, and his reason abdicated its throne. He was what you would call mentally unbalanced, as all men are who allow their false beliefs to obtain the ascendancy.

We must not place gangsters, assassins, and murderers in charge of our mind. Place Wisdom and Divine Love in charge of your mind. Let faith in God, and all things good take charge of your mind. The subjective or subconscious mind within each of us is of tremendous importance and significance, but it can be influenced negatively and positively. Be sure that you influence it only positively, constructively, and harmoniously. The subconscious possesses transcendent powers, but it is at the same time amenable to good and bad suggestions. The explanations which I gave him made a profound impression on him.

I gave him the following written prayer which he was to repeat for ten or fifteen minutes three or four times a day: "God's Love, Truth, and Wisdom flood my mind and heart. I love the Truth, I hear the Truth, and I know the Truth. God's River of Peace floods my mind, and I give thanks for my freedom."

He repeated the above prayer slowly, quietly, reverently, and with deep feeling, particularly prior to sleep. By identifying with harmony and peace, he brought about a rearrangement of the thought-patterns and imagery of his mind, and a healing followed. He knew that what was true of God was true of himself. He brought about a conviction by repetition, faith, and expectancy.

My prayer for him night and morning was as follows: "John is thinking rightly. He is reflecting Divine Wisdom and Divine Intelligence in all ways. His mind is the perfect mind of God, unchanging and eternal. He hears the Voice of God which is the Voice of Peace and Love. He understands the Truth, he knows the Truth, and he loves the Truth. God's River of Peace floods his mind. His mind is full of God's Wisdom and Understanding. Whatever is vexing him now is leaving him, and I pronounce him free and at peace."

I meditated on these words of Truth night and morning, getting the "feel" of peace and harmony; at the end of a week this young man was completely free. I fasted from the poisoned feast of sense-evidence and fear-symptoms. I had to cure myself of the belief in a diseased state, and outer results necessarily followed. I think my explanation was a great help to this young man. The ill state is conditioned in us as long as we see that state of illness portrayed. Our failure is due to absence of faith in the disciples (our mental faculties). We must contemplate the Infinite Perfection within us, and keep on doing so, until the day breaks and the shadows flee away.

He suffered not the demons to speak.

Chapter

2

How Your Mind Heals the Sick

And he arose out of the synagogue, and entered into Simon's house. And Simon's wife's mother was taken with a great fever; and they besought him for her. And he stood over her, and rebuked the fever; and it left her: and immediately she arose and ministered unto them. Luke 4:38-39. Related passage, Matt. 8:14-15.

Some time ago, a woman told me her child had a very high fever and was not expected to live. The doctor had prescribed small doses of aspirin, and had administered an antibiotic preparation. The mother was involved in a contemplated divorce action and was terribly agitated and emotionally disturbed. This disturbed feeling was communicated subconsciously to the child, and naturally the child got ill.

Children are at the mercy of their parents and are controlled by the dominant mental atmosphere of those around them. They have not yet reached the age of reason where they can take control of their own thoughts, emotions, and reactions to life. This mother, at my suggestion, decided to get quiet and still by reading the *Twenty-third Psalm*, praying for guidance, also praying for the peace and harmony of her husband, and pouring out love upon him instead of resentment and rage. The fever of the child was the suppressed anger and rage of the mother which was felt by the child and expressed as a high fever, or a state of excitation of the mind.

Having quieted her own mind, she began to pray for the child in this manner: "Spirit which is God is the life of my child. Spirit has no temperature; it is never sick or feverish. The peace of God floods my child's mind and body. The Harmony, Health, Love, and Perfection of God are made manifest in my child's mind and body now. She is relaxed and at ease, poised, serene, and calm. I am now stirring up the gift of God within her, and all is well."

She repeated the above prayer slowly, quietly, and lovingly for about ten minutes. She noticed a remarkable change in the child, who awakened, and asked for a doll and for something to eat. The temperature became normal. What happened? The fever left the child because the mother was no longer feverish or agitated in her mind. Her mood of peace, harmony, and love was instantaneously felt by the child, and a corresponding reaction was produced in the child. She took her child by the hand, biblically speaking.

The *hand* means the Power of God. With the hand you fashion, mold, shape, and direct. It is symbolic of the Creative Power or Intelligence in all of us. She lifted her child by the *hand* in the sense that she lifted up the idea of health, harmony, and peace in her mind to the point of acceptance, and the Power of the Almighty responded accordingly. It is the nature of the Deeper Mind to respond to the nature of your thought. When the mother focused her attention on the idea of perfect health for her child, the Power of the Almighty flowed through her focal point of attention, and a healing followed.

When the Bible speaks of *entering into Simon's house*, it refers to what you are hearing. The word *Simon* means to hear, and *Simon's wife's mother* means the emotional state which follows what you have been hearing or giving attention to. If disturbed by some news, or if you become unduly excited, you must rise up in your *synagogue* (mind); i.e., you should contemplate the Inner Presence as saturating every atom of your being. Then a wave of inner peace will follow, and all will be well. You *rebuke the fever* or sick state by contemplating the Omnipresence of God. This is Divine Science in action.

Great peace have they who love thy law and nothing shall offend them.

And it came to pass, when he was in a certain city, behold a man full of leprosy: who seeing Jesus fell on his face, and besought him, saying, Lord, if thou wilt, thou canst make me clean. And he put forth his hand, and touched him, saying, I will: be thou clean. And immediately the leprosy departed from him. And he charged him to tell no man; but go, and shew thyself to the priest, and offer for thy cleansing, according as Moses commanded, for a testimony unto them. Luke 5:12-14. *Related passages,* Mark 1:40-44. Matt. 8:2-4.

A leper, biblically speaking, is a person who through erroneous thoughts has separated himself from the real Source of life. It means a man who is governed by the five senses, and is psychologically and spiritually separated from his Divine Center. A leprous or impure condition is the result of being governed by the five senses with its fears, superstitions, and erroneous thoughts.

He put forth his hand, and touched him, saying, I will: be thou clean. You have seen men lay hands on people, and pray over them, and a healing followed; this has occurred from time immemorial. Sometimes people refer to the man who practices the laying on of hands as a "natural born healer." Of course, we are all "natural born healers" for the simple reason that the Healing Presence of God is within all men. All of us can contact it with our thoughts. It responds to all. The Healing Principle is in the dog, the cat, the tree, and the bird. It is Omnipresent and is the Life of all things.

There are different degrees of faith. There is the man who, through faith, heals his ulcers, and another who heals a deep-seated, so-called incurable malignancy. It is as easy for the Healing Presence to heal a tubercular lung as a cut in the finger. There is no great or small in the God that made us all; there is no big or little, nor hard or easy. Omnipotence is within all men. The prayers of the man who lays his hand on another appeals to the cooperation of the unconscious; a response takes place, and *according to your faith* (feeling) *is it done unto you.* This is the time-honored procedure of healing.

And he charged him to tell no man. It is a wise procedure to refrain from going around telling everyone you had a spiritual healing. Many of your friends will pass derogatory and skeptical remarks which might undermine your faith, causing you to doubt and hence undo the benefits you received from the prayers of the healer and your own mental acceptance.

Shew thyself to the priest. When you pray, you are the *priest* offering up the *sacrifice.* Your feeling, mood, or attitude of receptivity is the connecting link between the Invisible and the visible. Your desire is your *offering;* you cleanse yourself by forgiving everyone, by sincerely wishing for all those who may have seemed to hurt you all of God's blessings such as peace, love, joy, and happiness. Having cleansed your mind of all impurities (negative imagery and destructive thoughts), you offer your gift (desire) to God by galvanizing yourself into the feeling of being one with your ideal. Become engrossed and absorbed in the joy of having heard the good news, or the joy of the answered prayer; this consumes the old state and gives birth to the new.

If you want a healing of your body, withdraw mentally from symptoms and evidence of senses and begin to think of God's Healing Presence within you. The five outward senses are now turned inward and focused on health and harmony. All your attention is on your health and peace of mind. The Almighty Creative Power flows through the focal point of attention. You feel the response of the Spirit flowing through you. The Healing Presence touches every atom of your being and you are spiritually enriched. Dwelling in conscious communion with the Divine, man oftentimes becomes intoxicated with the Spirit. A state of exhilaration of the whole being takes place. This spiritual awakening builds up the entire man, makes him new, so that each day adds a new joy. As we continue to pray scientifically, we are lifted up so that an outpouring of Spirit takes place, and our whole being is revivified and recharged.

Dr. Alexis Carrel, in *Man, The Unknown,* points out the marvelous effects produced by prayer. He cites a case of a cancerous sore which shriveled to a scar in front of his eyes. He recounts seeing wound-lesions heal in a few seconds, and pathological symptoms disappear in a few hours. Extreme activation of the processes of organic repair had set in. These healings of tumors, bums, etc., were due to nothing more than the release of the Healing Power within each one. God or Infinite Intelligence is the only Healer, the only Presence, the only Power. When we call on this Presence within, giving it supreme recognition, claiming that the Healing Power saturates our mind and body, we receive a corresponding flood of the Healing Power which permeates every atom of our body, cicatrizing wounds and making us whole. Our body begins to function harmoniously; its atomic and molecular formation once more is transformed into the way it is in the Divine Center within us; then we know the truth of the saying, *yet in my flesh shall I see God.*

When the Bible says, *offer for thy cleansing, according as Moses commanded,* you are to look at the word *Moses,* as Troward points out, as the Law—the way your deeper mind works. As you exalt your thought-patterns claiming and affirming your good, your deeper mind (the Law) automatically responds to the new mental pattern and mental imagery and a healing follows. The Law holds no grudges, no more so than the law of electricity. All you do is conform to the principle of electricity and results follow. You may have misused the principle for making water for fifty years; the moment you follow the correct procedure, you will get water.

And, behold, men brought in a bed a man which was taken with a palsy: and they sought means to bring him in, and to lay him before him. And when they could not find by what way they might bring him in because of the multitude, they went upon the housetop, and let him down through the tiling with his couch into the midst before Jesus. And when he saw their faith, he said unto him, Man, thy sins are forgiven thee. Luke 5:18-20. *Related passage,* Mark 2:3-5.

I say unto thee, Arise, and take up thy couch, and go into thine house. Luke 5:24.

I remember a case of palsy and tremors being treated some

21

years ago. The man's legs would become locked so that inability to move was experienced. Panic would ensue, and the man would be frozen to the spot even in the middle of a busy street. This condition of constant fear, panic, and foreboding was wearing him down. The following procedure was adopted. The first step was to get him out of nature's way. After *agreeing quickly with thy adversary* he was told he must not continue in a state of quarrel, fear, and panic as to why he was beset with such a physical condition, causes which brought it about, etc. He admitted to himself that the condition was present and quite a problem, but that he didn't have to have it. He said to himself, "I am going to deny the worst and return to the Rock from whence I came."

He turned to the God-Presence within which created him and knew what to do. This Healing Presence is Omnipresent, Omniscient, and Omnipotent. He aligned himself with the Infinite, realizing that the Healing Presence was saturating every atom of his being and flowing through him as harmony, health, peace, wholeness, and perfection. As he gradually filled his mind with these Eternal Verities, he became reconditioned to health and harmony. As he changed his mind, he changed his body, for the body is a shadow of the mind.

The Bible story says *men brought in a bed a man which was taken with a palsy.* The *bed* in which a man lies is his own mind. He lies down there with fear, doubt, condemnation, guilt, and superstition. These thoughts paralyze the mind and body.

In *Mark* 2:1-12 where we have a slightly different version of the same story, it says the man was *borne of four.* The numeral four represents the manifested world, the objective manifestation of subjective states of consciousness. *Four* means termination, the end result, the completion of a cycle of consciousness, negative or positive.

We are told that Jesus (awareness of the Power of God) healed him by *forgiving his sins. To sin* is to miss the mark, the goal of health, of happiness, of peace. We forgive ourselves by identifying mentally and emotionally with our ideal and continuing to do so until it jells within us as a conviction or subjective embodiment. We are, of course, sinning also when we think negatively or I when we resent, hate, condemn, or fear another person. If we think there is some power to challenge the One Power (God), we are also sinning because we are cohabiting mentally with evil, thereby attracting all manner of calamity, trouble, and loss. We sin when we deviate or turn away from your announced goal or aim in life which should always be peace, harmony, wisdom, and perfect health. To indulge in morbid imagery and destructive thoughts, we mar our happiness and miss the target of a full and happy life.

Jesus forgave the paralytic by saying, *Arise, and take up thy couch*, which means that Truth or God never judges or condemns. The Absolute does not judge—all judgment is given to the son. All men are sons of the Infinite. Your mind is the son or offspring of the Spirit; with that mind you claim, choose, select, and arrive at decisions and conclusions. If you err in your judgment or decision, you experience the automatic or compulsory reaction from your unconscious mind. Your mind is always forgiving you, because the moment you present it with new mental imagery and lovely patterns of thought, it responds accordingly. It is perpetually forgiving you; this is called the love of God or the mercy of God.

The paralytic could not be cured until his sins had been cancelled; but once the inner state of mind is changed through contact with the Healing Power and his sense of oneness with it, he now rises through the Power of the Almighty (the One Power) and he no longer is carried around by four men, symbolic of worldly beliefs and erroneous impressions of all kinds. The outer change conforms to the inner, spiritual awakening.

And when they could not find by what way they might bring him in because of the multitude, they went upon the housetop. The *multitude* refers to man's mental accusers such as fear, self-accusation, remorse, and condemnation. When he realizes that Truth or God or the law of life never condemns, he ceases to condemn and forgives himself. Then instead of lying down prone in a bed of false beliefs and fears of all kinds, through his contact with the Almighty Power he stands upright in the law, visioning and imagining his perfect health and wholeness.

You must go on the *housetop* if you want an answer to your prayer. You must climb. You do this by reminding yourself of the One Omnipotent Power and your faith in it. We climb by faith; we soar aloft above our problem with wings of faith and disciplined imagination. Faith means to look up to the One, giving all your allegiance, devotion, and loyalty to God. Truth means to go in one direction only, knowing that the Great Physician is within, that He is healing you now, and that there is none to oppose, challenge, or thwart Him in any way. Fear is a denial of God and is nothing but a conglomeration of sinister shadows, without reality and with nothing to sustain it.

It is said they climbed up and opened the roof and let the paralytic down through the roof before Jesus. All this means is that in contemplating God and His Holy Presence, you are lifted up, your mind is open and receptive, and you let your deep, abiding conviction in the idea of perfect health sink down to subliminal levels within you. Jesus means God is your deliverer, the I AM within you, which receives the impress of your conviction and responds accordingly. If you break the roof of a house, you can see the heavens above, the sun, moon, and stars. Don't let the press of worldly thoughts prevent you from receiving a healing. If your loved one is sick, open up the roof of your mind and let in the Healing Light, surrender your loved one to God and realize that he is now immersed in the Holy Omnipresence; see him as he ought to be, radiant, happy, and free. Claim what's true of God is true of your loved one. As you continue to do this, your loved one will rise up from his bed of pain, misery, and suffering, and walk the earth glorifying God.

And it came to pass also on another sabbath, that he entered into the synagogue and taught: and there was a man whose right hand was withered. And the scribes and Pharisees watched him, whether he would heal on the sabbath day: that they might find an accusation against him. But he knew their thoughts, and said to the man, which had the withered hand, Rise up, and stand forth in the midst. And he arose and stood forth. Luke 6:6-8.

And looking round about upon them all, he said unto the man, Stretch forth thy hand. And he did so: and his hand was restored whole as the other. Luke 6:10. *Related passage,* Mark 3:3-5.

Elsie H. Salmon, a Missionary's wife in South Africa, tells in her book *He Heals Today* about a child with a deformed left hand. Three fingers were missing and in their place were tiny stumps. After prayer there was a growth of the whole hand at the end of the arm, and they began to unfold like a flower in front of their eyes. She also states that there is absolutely no doubt in the minds of people who have followed developments that a perfect hand is forming.

We must not look upon this as miraculous or something supernatural. We must begin to realize that the Creative Power which forms, molds, and shapes the body can certainly grow a hand, a leg, or an eye. After all where do the organs of our body come from? If you made an ice-box, couldn't you fix it if it were out of order, or if broken, couldn't you mend it and supply the missing parts? When Jesus said, *Stretch forth thy hand,* you must look upon it as a drama taking place in your own consciousness. You are Jesus in action when you know that the realization of your desire would save you from any predicament, be it what it may. You are Jesus or the spiritual man in action when your conscious and subconscious mind agree on the realization of your wish or prayer. When there is no further argument, and you have reached an agreement, you are Jesus Christ in action. Jesus represents your illumined reason, and Christ means the power and wisdom resident in your subjective self.

Elsie H. Salmon's faith in the Creative Power of God to form a new hand for a child caused the stunted arm to grow. Her faith is her savior or her Jesus. She is aware of the reality of what she prays for and knows that the nature of the Infinite Intelligence is responsiveness.

In the correct esoteric interpretation of the Bible, it must be understood that principles are personified as persons in order to make portrayal and interaction vivid and forceful. *Know ye not your own selves, how that Jesus Christ is in you, except ye be reprobates?* 2 Cor. 13:5.

We must not however confine the story of the man with the withered hand to its literal meaning. *The hand* is a symbol of power, of direction, of effectiveness. With your hand you fashion, mold, create, and design. The hand of the Almighty means the Creative Power of God focused or directed on some objective. Symbolically a man has a *withered hand* when he has an inferiority complex, feels guilty, inadequate, or is a defeatist. Such a man does not function efficiently and is not expressing his God-given powers.

We *stretch forth our hand* when we release our Hidden Power and become channels for Divine Love, Light, Truth, and Beauty.

His hand was restored whole as the other means a healthy, happy, well balanced, and wholesome personality. Numbers of people are sick, unhappy, dissatisfied, inept, and inefficient. Their attitude toward life is all wrong; moreover their work is shoddy and desultory. They do not sing in their hearts at their work. Whenever you turn with confidence and trust to the Almighty Power within knowing that you are guided, directed by this Inner Light, and that you are expressing yourself fully, you will actually become a channel for the Divine and you will move from glory to glory.

The dreams, ambitions, ideals, plans, and purposes of many are withered and frozen in the mind because they do not know how to bring them to pass. The external world denies their desire. Not knowing the laws of mind and how to pray scientifically, they find their wonderful ideas die aborning in their minds, resulting in frustration and neurosis. If you look around you in your office or factory, you will see many people with a *withered hand*. They are stagnating, literally dying on the vine. Life is progressive, life is growth. There is no end to our unfoldment or creativeness. We wither our hand (our ability to achieve and accomplish) by saying, "If I had Joe's brains or his wealth . . . his connections . . . I could advance and be somebody. But look at me, just a nobody. I was born on the wrong side of the tracks. I must be satisfied with my lot. I have a withered hand."

This is the way many people talk. They are constantly demoting and depreciating themselves. Liquidate, banish, and eradicate from your mind fear, doubt, and ill-will. Trust God completely, go all the way out on a limb and say with feeling and humility, "I can do all things through the God-Power and Awareness which strengthens, guides, comforts, and directs me." Watch the wonders you will perform. *Stretch forth your hand* by enlarging your concept or estimate of yourself. Aim high, raise your sights, realize you will always go where your vision is. You will be *stretching forth your hand* as you get a picture in your mind of what you wish to achieve. Touch this with faith in the God-Wisdom to bring it forth and you will see it made manifest on the screen of space. You will be satisfied for awhile; then a divine discontent will stir you again, causing you to aim higher and higher and so on to infinity.

To *stretch forth your hand*, when psychologically understood, is the soundest, simplest, and most wonderful philosophy any man can have.

I say unto you now, *Stretch forth thy hand*.

Chapter

3

ABSENT TREATMENT AND
THE HEALING OF INSANITY

And when he was now not far from the house, the centurion sent friends to him, saying unto him, Lord, trouble not thyself: for I am not worthy that thou shouldest enter under my roof: Wherefore neither thought I myself worthy to come unto thee: but say in a word, and my servant shall be healed. For I also am a man set under authority, having under me soldiers, and I say unto one, Go, and he goeth: and to another, Come, and he cometh: and to my servant, Do this, and he doeth it. When Jesus heard these things, he marveled at him, and turned him about, and said unto the people that followed him, I say unto you, I have not found so great faith, no, not in Israel. And they that were sent, returning to the house, found the servant whole that had been sick. Luke 7:6-10. *Related passages,* Matt. 8:5-13. John 4:46-53.

Here is the technique of absent treatment portrayed in a beautiful and simple way. You are told how to pray for another or send your *word* and heal him. When you pray for another, or give what is termed a mental and spiritual treatment, you simply correct what you hear and see in your mind by knowing and feeling the other's freedom. Faith comes to you as you leave the literal interpretation of life and enter into the psychological, spiritual interpretation of life.

Many of you, like the author, were no doubt in the United States Army and you know how to take orders. A soldier is conditioned to obey implicitly his superior officers. After considerable training the soldier becomes disciplined; i.e., his mind and body are definitely bent to certain actions. The officer is a man of authority. He has learned to command, but first he had to learn to take orders himself; and he, too, is subject to authority from his superiors.

When you pray for another, you must be a good soldier; you must learn how to stand at attention and follow the order, "Eyes right." You must give attention to the spiritual values or Truths of life and keep your "eyes right" by seeing (spiritual perception) the other as he ought to be, happy, peaceful, and free. You must begin to discipline your thoughts, feelings, emotions, and faculties.

You know very well that you can begin now as you read these lines. If your thoughts wander, bring them back and say to them, "I told you to give attention to health, peace," or whatever it is you are concentrating on.

The servants are your thoughts, ideas, moods, feelings, and attitudes of mind. They serve you nobly or ignobly, depending on the orders you issue. If you are an employer, you may order the employees to do certain things in the store. You expect them to obey; you are paying them to conform to your business methods and processes. In the same manner, you order your thoughts around. You are the master, not the serf or slave. Surely you do not and will not permit the gangster-thoughts of hate, fear, prejudice, jealousy, rage, etc., to order you around and make a football of you.

When you begin to discipline your mind, you do not permit doubt, anxiety, and false impressions of the world to browbeat, intimidate, and push you around. You are conditioning your mind so that you definitely issue orders to your thoughts to give attention to your aims in life, to your ideals; likewise, you direct and channel all your emotions constructively. You have complete dominion.

You can't visualize an emotion. You must remember that emotion follows thought; and when you control your thoughts and mental imagery, you are in charge of your emotions.

No person, place, or thing can annoy you, disturb you, or

hurt you—they do not have that authority. For example, another could call you a skunk. Are you a skunk? No. The suggestions or statements of the other could not affect you except through your thought. This is the only emotional power you have. Your thought in such an instance could be, "God's peace fills that man's mind." You are in charge of the movement of your mind. You can move in anger, hate, or revenge; also, you can move in peace, harmony, and good will.

The disciplined mind is accustomed to take a spiritual medicine called "In tune with the Infinite." The moment you are tempted to react negatively, identify immediately with your aim. Switch to your ideal immediately and you have overcome and are victorious. You are a man of authority, and you say to your thoughts (servants) *go and they go, come and they come.*

You can give your faculty of imagination to anything you wish, such as lack, loss, or misfortune.

You can discipline, direct, and focus your imagination on success, health, and prosperity also. What you imagine and feel as true comes to pass. Let your imagination become the workshop of God, which is what it should be.

Let me cite the misuse of imagination. A mother whose son is rather late arriving home begins to imagine that he has met with some disaster. She sees in her vivid, distorted, twisted mind mental pictures of him on a hospital cot or she dramatizes an accident in her imagination. She can *send her word and heal him* and herself also. She must learn how to pray scientifically and become a good soldier who follows orders.

You are under *Holy Orders* when you pray. You have surrendered your ego and intellectual pride in your own thoughts, viewpoints, and perspective, yielding to the God-Wisdom within. You are under orders now to bring forth harmony, health, peace, joy, wholeness, and beauty in the world. You are here to let your light shine. You must have faith and complete trust in the Omnipotence, Omniscience, and Boundless Love of the Infinite which seeks only to express itself. Identify yourself mentally and

31

emotionally with God. You feel and know that you are a channel for the manifestation of all of God's attributes, qualities, and potencies, and that God flows through you as harmony, health, peace, joy, and abundance. As you make a habit of this kind of prayer by frequently repeating or affirming these Truths, your mind will become imbued with Eternal Verities, and you will find yourself under a Divine compulsion to bring forth only the good, the beautiful, and the true. You have placed yourself under *Holy Orders*, or Orders of the Only One—God. You become a God-directed man, a divinely ordained person whose sole mission in the world is to follow the orders of the *Holy One who inhabiteth Eternity whose name is perfect.*

Whose orders are you carrying out? *Ye are servants to whom ye yield yourself, servants to obey.* Whatever idea I yield to, or give myself to, will dominate, control, and compel me to act it out as frustration and expression.

In the above instance, whose order do you think the woman was obeying when she had all kinds of misgivings about her boy—bombarding him with a barrage of negation and with dire forebodings which if continued would have had catastrophic implications? This woman was taking her orders from the thoughts of fear, worry, and anxiety. In other words the marauders and intruders in her mind were browbeating her and making her a nervous wreck.

Begin now to *stretch forth your hand* by realizing there is no limit to your possibilities. Feel and believe God is your Silent Partner, counseling, directing, and governing you. As you do this, your life will be wonderful and satisfying. It will be more useful and constructive than it is. Begin to know yourself. Try the amazing power of true prayer as outlined in each chapter of this book. As you yield yourself to the God-Wisdom, you will live a better life than you ever dreamed of.

Arise, take up thy bed (new mental attitude) *and walk* the earth radiant, happy, and free.

Now when he came nigh to the gate of the city, behold, there was a dead man carried out, the only son of his mother, and she was a widow: and much people of the city was with her. And when the Lord saw her, he had compassion on her, and said unto her, Weep not. And he came and touched the bier: and they that bare him stood still. And he said, Young man, I say unto thee, Arise. And he that was dead sat up and began to speak. Luke 7:12-15.

Here is a wonderful, psychological drama. The *dead man* is your desire which you have failed to manifest. As you claim you now are what you long to be, you are resurrecting the *dead man* within you.

According to your belief is it done unto you. To believe something is to accept it as true. We are told the dead man was the son of a widow. A *widow* is a woman whose husband is dead. When we are not married, mentally and emotionally, to God and His truths, we are truly dead to peace, joy, health, happiness, and inspiration. A true widow is one whose husband is God, or the Good, and who is not governed by sense-evidence and worldly belief. The *son,* the desire, of such a woman will not remain dead because she turns to her Lord, which is the Creative Power within her and, with the door of her five senses closed, she completely rejects all that her senses deny. Silently and lovingly she claims and feels herself to be what she longs to be, knowing in her heart that her Lord (the Spirit within) will honor and validate her claim. She lives, moves, and has her being in the mental atmosphere of complete acceptance; as she continues to qualify her consciousness in this way, she reaches an inner conviction, thereby resurrecting the *dead man* within her. Her inner mood of triumph is her *Lord* commanding the *dead man. Young man, I say unto thee, Arise.*

This is the external manifestation of her subjective embodiment or the joy of the answered prayer. Whatever we appropriate and assimilate in consciousness, we resurrect. When it says the *dead man sat up and began to speak,* it means that when your prayer is answered you speak in a new tongue. The sick man who is healed speaks in the tongue of joyous health and exudes an inner radiance. Our dead hopes and desires speak when we bear witness to our inner beliefs and assumptions.

As a corollary to this, I would like to relate about a young man I saw in Ireland a few years ago. He was a distant relative. He was in a comatose condition; his kidneys had not functioned for two days. I went to see him accompanied by one of his brothers. I knew he was a devout Roman Catholic and I said to him, "Jesus is right here now and you see him. He is putting his hand out and is this moment laying His hands on you."

I repeated this several times, slowly, gently, and positively. He was unconscious when I spoke and was not consciously aware of the presence of any of us. He sat up in bed, opened his eyes, and said, "Jesus was here; I know I am healed; I shall live."

What happened? This man's unconscious mind accepted my statement that Jesus was there and his subconscious projected that thought form; i.e., this man's concept of Jesus was portrayed based on what he saw in church statues, paintings, etc. He believed Jesus was there in the flesh and that he had placed his hands upon him.

The readers of this book are well aware of the fact that you can tell a man in a trance that his grandfather is here now and that he will see him clearly. He will see what he believes to be his grandfather. His subconscious projects the image of his grandfather based on his subconscious, memory picture. You can give the same man a posthypnotic suggestion saying to him, "When you come out of the trance, you will greet your grandfather and talk to him."

He does exactly that. This is called a subjective hallucination. The faith kindled in the unconscious of my Catholic relative, based on his firm belief that Jesus came to heal him, was the healing factor. It is always done unto us according to our faith or mental conviction.

The subconscious is amenable to suggestion even though the subject is unconscious; the deeper mind can receive and act upon the suggestion of the operator. In a sense you could call such an incident the *resurrection of the dead*. It is the resurrection of health, faith, confidence, and vitality. We must never let hope, joy, peace, love, and faith in God die in us; that state of mind is the real death. We should die to fear, ignorance, jealousy, envy, hate, etc. We should starve these states to death by neglect. When fear dies, there is only room for faith. When hate dies, there is only room for love. When ignorance dies, there is only room for wisdom.

Now it came to pass on a certain day, that he went into a ship with his disciples: and he said unto them, Let us go over unto the other side of the lake. And they launched forth. But as they sailed he fell asleep: and there came down a storm of wind on the lake: and they were filled with water, and were in jeopardy. And they came to him, and awoke him, saying, Master, master, we perish. Then he arose, and rebuked the wind and the raging of the water: and they ceased, and there was a calm. Luke 8:2224.

Here we are told how to control our emotions and heal the turbulent soul. This is a story of everyone, not just about men in a ship, because we are always traveling somewhere psychologically speaking. When beset with a difficulty, we seek an answer, a solution. When fearful, we must move to faith. The journey is always first in the mind—the body follows where the mind goes. The body cannot do anything or go any place unless the mind agrees and directs. Consciousness is the only power and the only mover. The consciousness of man is perpetual motion. Our mind is always active, even when asleep.

Our *disciples* are our mental attitudes, moods, and faculties which go with us wherever we go. We must not let *Jesus go to sleep in the boat.* In order to understand the science of life in the Bible, you must *regard*—*Jesus,* the *boat,* the *wind,* the *waves,* and the *disciples,* as personifications of truths, faculties, moods, and thoughts of mankind. Your *Jesus* is your awareness of the Divine Power within you, enabling you to achieve, accomplish, and realize your objectives. Your knowledge of the laws of mind and your use of mental and spiritual laws is your *savior* or solution at all times, everywhere.

You must not permit *Jesus to sleep in the boat,* which means you must not go blithely along with the winds (opinions of man) and waves (fears, doubts, envy, hatred, etc.) of the race mind. The *lake* is your mind; when your mind is at peace, God's wisdom and

God's ideas rise to the surface of your mind. The mind that stays on God feels God's River of Peace flowing through it and is full of poise, balance, and serenity. The *Storm* of *wind* represent the fear, terror, and anguish which seize man at times, causing him to vacillate, hesitate, and tremble with anxiety. He finds himself pulled two ways; his fear holds him back and prevents him from going forward.

What do you do when fear and limitation seize your mind? Realize that when you are looking at your desire, you see your *savior* or the solution in your mind. Your *savior* is always knocking at the door of your mind. Perhaps you are working for the government and you are saying, "Oh, I can't make any more money; I've reached the maximum." You are now seeing the *waters* of confusion and doubt welling up in you. Don't become submerged in these watery, negative emotions. Wake up your *savior*, stir up the gift of God within you.

Do it in this way. Realize first of all that the wish, desire, ideal, plan, or purpose you want to realize is definitely a reality of the mind, though invisible; then realize that by uniting with your desire mentally, you can definitely and positively move over the turbulent, noisy, and foaming waters of fear and hesitancy. Your faith is your feeling and your awareness that the thing you are praying for is a reality of the mind in the form of an idea or desire. Inasmuch as you thought about it, it is real. Trust the mental picture; it is real. By contemplating its reality you *walk over the waters* and you *quiet the waves* of fear. Your fear has abated because you know that when you focus your attention on your ideal, the Creative Power of God flows through that focal point of attention. You are now *stilling the waves*. You have disciplined your mind. You have reasoned it out and you know that the idea is always real. The thought is *the substance of things hoped for, the evidence of things not seen,* for the simple reason that you believe in the possibility of the execution of the idea.

Keep your eyes on your goal, your objective, knowing in your heart that there is an Almighty Power which supports you in all your ways. It never deserts you or leaves you. The subjective mind responds to your constructive thinking and feeling; thereby sustenance, strength, and power are given you. To look down at the *waves* of fear, false belief, and error is to sink. Look up and you will go where your vision is. Your ordered mind, your faith, and confidence enable you to walk over all the waters of life to *green pastures and still waters.* You can *command the winds and waves,* and they will obey.

And when he went forth to land, there met him out of the city a certain man, which had devils long time, and ware no clothes, neither abode in any house, but in the tombs. When he saw Jesus, he cried out, and fell down before him, and with a loud voice said, What have I to do with thee, Jesus, thou Son of God most high? I beseech thee, torment me not. (For he had commanded the unclean spirit to come out of the man. For oftentimes it had caught him: and he was kept bound with chains and in fetters; and he brake the bands, and was driven of the devil into the wilderness.) And Jesus asked him, saying, What is thy name? And he said, Legion: because many devils were entered into him. And they besought him that he would not command them to go out into the deep. And there was there an herd of many swine feeding on the mountain: and they besought him that he would suffer them to enter into them. And he suffered them. Then went the devils out of the man, and entered into the swine: and the herd ran violently down a steep place into the take, and were choked. When they that fed them saw what was done, they fled, and went and told it in the city and in the country. Then they went out to see what was done; and came to Jesus, and found the man, out of whom the devils were departed, sitting at the feet of Jesus, clothed, and in his right mind: and they were afraid, Luke 8:27-35. *Related passages,* Matt. 8:28-32. Mark 5:1-13.

In reading this account, it certainly reminds you of a manic-depressive type of psychosis. This is, of course, a form of mental derangement and is characterized by combativeness and destructivity. In the book of *Mark* we have a story similar to the above wherein the maniac is depicted as *living among the tombs.*

The *tombstones* are a record of the dead, which means here that the man is living in the dead past, nursing some old grudge or grievance until it becomes an obsession in his mind. The madman is a man who has allowed or permitted the gangsters of remorse, hate, revenge, or self-pity to take charge of his reasoning, discriminating mind. We must never abdicate and let destructive, negative emotions control us. Emotion follows thought; and by redirecting our thought life, we control our emotional life. Man cannot visualize an emotion. He has to construct the scene or event in his mind and relive it, thereby generating the emotion. In psychiatry the doctors endeavor to correct the basic conflicts of the patient and give him a new orientation.

Jesus addressing the insane man asks, *What is thy name; And he said, Legion: because many devils were entered into him.* I knew a man in New York who feared that whenever he went into a bar that some evil entity was lurking in the shadows somewhere to take possession of him. I don't know where he heard or read of such rank superstition. This belief governed his mind and caused all kinds of trouble. His subjective mind, being dominated by this all-potent but false suggestion, gained control of his reasoning faculties and his reason abdicated. He had to experience the effects of such a false belief; this subjective false belief gained the ascendancy. He began to hear what he supposed to be spirit voices, not knowing he was talking to himself. He thought he was conversing with supernatural entities. He began to realize that his subconscious mind was simply acting in obedience to the false suggestions of fear and belief in spirits which he had dwelt upon so long. The subconscious will assume a dozen different characters whose collective name is *Legion.* This man went to a clergyman who used the ritual of the Church to banish the tormentors. The procedure of the exorcist was, as the reader will readily conclude, a series of incantations or adjurations in the name of Jesus Christ, The ritual, ceremony, and prayers of the exorcist instilled great faith and confidence in the subconscious mind of the man. He was very receptive to the power of the Church and the priest to cast out his so-called devils. The exorcist had confidence in what he was doing also. This coupled with the faith of the so-called possessed man brought about a marvelous healing. The priceless ingredient in the whole process was simply faith, which brought about a basic change in the mental attitude of the patient that generated a healing. It was, of course, blind faith which is certainly better than no faith at all. The bones of saints, certain waters, the incantations of a witch doctor may affect the deeper mind and cause a psychological transformation inducing faith and receptivity.

Divine healing or Spiritual healing refers to the harmonious functioning of our conscious and subconscious minds. Our mind contains within its conscious and subconscious areas all our desires, characteristics, tendencies, and urges with which we were born. Through the process of thinking, education, and experience we have acquired many attitudes and habits of various kinds. Man is a creature of habit. When we begin to think intelligently we deliberately reject all negative thoughts and opinions. When we fail to realize a desire or ideal, we become full of fear and frustration, this leads to unconscious impressions. These repressed urges and tendencies seek expression and an outlet. These destructive emotions manifest as inner conflicts; if those are not resolved, disorganization of the mentality takes place and a completely disordered mind is the result.

The subjective self in us is forever seeking to restore a balance in us; when our fears, tensions, and conflicts become unbearable, nature or the Divine Self in us causes us to lose all consciousness of the problems; this is called insanity. The mind is now deflected and detached from the strain and stress which caused the trouble. Imbalance results when we fail to choose between good and evil. We must not seek to solve our problems without Divine Wisdom and Divine Power. The mental derangement is simply the expression of deep, repressed urges and conflicts which are too great to bear. A complex is a group of ideas highly charged with emotion seeking expression. If a man is full of hatred and prejudice, he is living in *the tombs*. When these are exposed and held up to the light of reason, they are dissipated. In Bible language, you are Jesus casting out the devils of hate, prejudice, and jealousy. These obnoxious complexes are always hiding in the *tomb* (subconscious mind). When men refuse to acknowledge and hold up their prejudices, peeves, and grudges to the light of reason, these ideas are forced down beneath the conscious level of personality and they are bound by the chains of fear, ignorance, and various mental obsessions. When we nurse grudges, prejudices, revenge, and remorse they sink into the unconscious area of mind like a smoldering fire ready to explode sooner or later. If we recognize these smoldering flames and handle them intelligently, we can be free and lead a normal life.

Our emotional side of life is the driving power. It would be a good thing for all of us to take a good look at ourselves and see if the qualities we criticize so harshly in others are not in ourselves. When our story says the insane man sat at the *feet* of the Master, it depicts our understanding of the laws of mind and how they work.

When you are asked to pray for an insane man in the hospital, you can't get his cooperation. He has ceased to reason and discriminate. Actually he is governed by the ghosts of the subconscious that walk the gloomy galleries of his mind. When you pray for such a type of person, it is necessary to do all the work yourself. You have to convince yourself of his freedom, peace, harmony, and understanding. You could pray two or three times a day in this way: "I now decree for John Doe that the intelligence, wisdom, and peace of God are made manifest in him and he is free, radiant, and happy. He is now clothed in his right mind. The Mind of God is the only Real and Eternal Mind; this is his mind, and he is poised, serene, calm, relaxed, and at ease. He is full of faith in God, in life, and all good things. I decree this, I feel it, and I see him whole and perfect now. Thank you, Father."

By repeating these Truths to yourself, realizing that there is but one mind, you will gradually, through frequent picturing in your mind, reach a dominant conviction; and the man you are praying for will at that moment be healed. In a case such as the above, all healing has to be done in the mind of the practitioner. The practitioner must not at any time give power to symptoms, or the prognosis of the case. He must rely exclusively on the operating Principle of Life which forever responds to his faith and trust in it. When you pray for another, you leave the realm of time and space, of appearances and circumstances, the verdict of the world, and you judge righteous judgment. This means that you come to a conclusion that the Inner Man (the Spiritual, Divine Presence) cannot be sick, confused, or insane. Nothing could ever happen to Wisdom, Peace, Harmony, Intelligence, or Divine Love. The inner man has all of these qualities and attributes, and the practitioner by meditating on the Eternal Life, perfect mind, and absolute peace of the mentally sick man, dissipates and dissolves the mist of fixed opinions and error thoughts that separate the man from God's River of Peace. Become aware now of the Almighty Power which is Invisible and Intangible. Don't struggle in your prayer-work; then you will find the outer coat of painting will fade away, and the masterpiece will be revealed in all its pristine glory.

The story says *the devils went out of the man and entered into the swine: and the herd ran violently down a steep place into the lake, and were choked.* Pigs were chosen symbolically as pigs decapitate themselves when swimming; likewise, when we begin to swim psychologically in the waters of life, our negative thoughts and confusions (devils) die from want of belief. The past dies for you when you no longer think of the past. If you feel you can't accomplish or cannot be healed, you are looking back at the past, you are living *among the tombs.* Don't listen to these messages of the past. The ideal or desire which beckons, which says to you, "Arise, go forth, achieve," is the savior walking down the corridors of your mind. Accept that ideal as real now and walk as though you possessed it. You are now *clothed* in your right mind, and a wave of peace moves over you because you realize that which you seek already is. This is why the Bible says, *Lift up your eyes, look on the fields; for they are already white to harvest.*

And, behold, there came a man named Jairus, and he was a ruler of the synagogue: and he fell down at Jesus' feet, and besought him that he would come into his house: For he had one only daughter, about twelve years of age, and she lay a dying. But as he went the people thronged him. And a woman having an issue of blood twelve years, which had spent all her living upon physicians, neither could be healed of any, came behind him, and touched the border of his garment: and immediately her issue of blood stanched. And Jesus said, Who touched me? When all denied, Peter and they that were with him said, Master, the multitude throng thee and press thee, and sayest thou, Who touched me? And Jesus said, Somebody hath touched me: for I perceive that virtue is gone out of me. And when the woman saw that she was not hid, she came trembling, and falling down before him, she declared unto him before all the people for what cause she had touched him, and how she was healed immediately. And he said unto her, Daughter, be of good comfort: thy faith hath made thee whole; go in peace. While he yet spake, there cometh one from the ruler of the synagogue's house, saying to him, Thy daughter is dead; trouble not the Master. But when Jesus heard it, he answered him, saying, Fear not: believe only, and she shall be made whole. And when he came into the house, he suffered no man to go in, save Peter, and James, and John, and the father and the mother of the maiden. And all wept, and bewailed her: but he said, Weep not; she is not dead, but sleepeth. And they laughed him to scorn, knowing that she was dead. And he put them all out, and took her by the hand, and called, saying, Maid, arise. And her spirit came again, and she arose straightway: and he commanded to give her meat. Luke 8:41-55. *Related passages,* Matt. 9:20-22, 14:35-36. Mark 5:28-34.

All these stories are psychological and must be interpreted as such. You *are Jairus* which means the ruling thought in the mind; *you throw yourself at Jesus' feet;* i.e., you begin to realize that based on your new understanding of the Power of God in you, you can resurrect the *dying child.* The *dying daughter* represents your unfulfilled ambition, the desire of your heart. *Jesus, Jairus,* the *daughter,* the *woman with the issue of blood, Peter, James,* and *John all* these characters are within each of us. It is a story of everyman. Our *daughter* (desire) *is dying* because we lack the faith to resurrect it. A *woman with the issue of blood* cannot give birth, she cannot conceive. A bleeding womb cannot possibly give form to a body. *Woman* means emotion, feeling. When our emotions are running wild and undisciplined, we are symbolically *bleeding from the womb.* Energy

42

and vitality are being wasted because of fear, worry, and doubt. The *womb* (mind) must be closed in order to procreate.

As you go within and shut the door of your senses to all objective evidence and assume that you are what you long to be, you are closing your *womb* (mind) and will succeed in giving form to your idea or plan. Your thought is creative; when you begin to think on what you wish to express, the Creative Power of God responds and by remaining faithful to the new mental focus, you will resurrect your *child*. You know in your heart that *the child is not dead* and that you can bring it forth. Your new attitude of mind which is your faith closes the *womb*.

Thy faith hath made thee whole. Faith comes through hearing that there is only One Sovereign and Supreme Power which can do all things for it is Almighty. As we give our attention to the Truth about this One Power, we are said to hear it. Let us hear the Truths about the Power of Love, faith, and good will, and let us trust our subjective wisdom to reveal to us the answer to any problem. Faith is going in one direction only. Many people give their ear or attention to lies, falsehoods, superstition, and erroneous concepts of all kinds. When we do this, confusion reigns supreme.

Somebody hath touched me: for I perceive that virtue is gone out of me. You can mentally and emotionally touch faith, love, joy, and peace. When you mentally appropriate the idea of perfect health, the Healing Presence responds, and you are made whole—this is the virtue that comes out of the depths of yourself.

We are told that *they laughed him to scorn.* Is it not true that your five senses mock and laugh at you? Do they not challenge you and say, "It can't be done," or "It is impossible." This is why you suspend your senses and direct your mind to give attention to the new mental picture, and as you envelop this desire with the mood of love, you become one with it. This is the meaning of taking *Peter, James, and John into the house with Him.* The *house* is your mind or consciousness. Your own I AM-NESS is the father and mother of all ideas, desires, concepts, and urges. *Peter* means faith in God; *James* means to judge righteously, i.e., to hear the good news only; *John* is love or a sense of atonement, at-one-ment, with your ideal. We actually take these three qualities with us whenever we recognize a state as true that is not evident to the senses. Our reason and senses may question, ridicule, scoff, and laugh, but if we will only go within, knowing that when we feel something as true, Omnipotence moves in our behalf; then, though the whole world would deny it, we would demonstrate our desire because we are sealed in faith, and *according to our faith is it done unto us.*

Chapter

4

YOUR HEALING PRESENCE

And, behold, a man of the company cried out, saying, Master, I beseech thee, look upon my son: for he is mine only child. And, lo, a spirit taketh him, and he suddenly crieth out; and it teareth him that he foameth again, and bruising him hardly departeth from him. And I besought thy disciples to cast him out; and they could not. And Jesus answering said, O faithless and perverse generation, how long shall I be with you, and suffer you? Bring thy son hither. And as he was yet a coming, the devil threw him down, and tare him. And Jesus rebuked the unclean spirit, and healed the child, and delivered him again to his father. And they were all amazed at the mighty power of God. Luke 9:38-43. *Related passages,* Matt. 17:14-21. Mark 9:17-29.

There are similar stories in the *Book of Mark* and *Matthew,* which definitely seem to indicate a disease known as epilepsy today. Of course, looking at the story literally one would think of demon possession which was the popular belief in those days. The boy is thrown down; he foams at the mouth and wallows on the ground suffering from convulsions. The Bible does not mention the word epilepsy. The word is derived from the Greek word *epilepsia,* which means a falling sickness characterized by seizures. The Greeks called epilepsy the sacred disease because it was believed to be caused by the moon. As we all know, the term lunatic comes from the Latin word *lunaticus.* In ancient symbology the moon meant the subconscious mind. The sun was the illumined intellect or the conscious mind full of wisdom.

In other words the Bible is saying the child had a subconscious poison pocket which was the cause of his seizures and epileptic fits. *The sun shall not smite thee by day, nor the moon by night.* Psalms. 121:6. Modern psychology and psychiatry show definitely that mental and physical disorders have their roots in the depths of the deeper mind, called the subconscious or unconscious.

Negative subconscious patterns are called *pestilences of the darkness.* By turning to the God-Presence within and calling on the Power and Goodness of God, we bring the action of God to play in our life. We prove our allegiance, devotion, and love for God by identifying ourselves with His qualities and by absolutely refusing to recognize evil as having any power over us. Because of our faith in the One Power, we claim His Perfect Harmony and Perfect Peace which is His Will.

Hippocrates, about 400 B.C., recognized this type of mental disorder called epilepsy which in his time was believed to be caused by divine beings. He ridicules the superstitions of his day and points out that the disease could not be of divine origin for the simple reason that the condition was healed by purifications and various incantations which were in vogue at the time. A local psychiatrist told me that his study of Hippocrates showed that this famous physician had a wonderful knowledge of the causes underlying mental disorders of all kinds.

Whether the child in question was an idiot child, deaf and dumb, or an epileptic doesn't matter. We must realize in praying for another that *with God all things are possible.* The *Book of Mark* says this type of case is healed by *prayer and fasting. Fasting* means, fasting from the sense evidence, symptoms, and race belief. We must *fast;* i.e., mentally reject the poisoned feast of objective evidences.

Where did this healing take place? Jesus, as the story goes, had to heal himself of the disease, whether insanity or idiocy, and outer results necessarily followed. It is the *prayer of faith* which gets results. The mentally deranged state of consciousness is conditioned in us as long as we see that condition of illness portrayed. The failure to heal an insane child or an idiot is not the child's fault but the absence of faith in the *disciples* (mind's faculties). The one praying must cure himself of the claim supposedly gripping the ailing child; the condition is actually gripping the practitioner who is unawakened yet to the Truth. When we fail in this type of case, we simply have failed to fix our mind's eye on the embodiment of health which the ailing one needs.

We are told the reason the disciples could not heal the sick boy was due to unbelief. There is a deep unconscious belief in the minds of people that certain diseases are difficult to heal; when they see a lunatic and his symptoms, their senses are deeply impressed with the difficulties. The *disciples* spoken of are our own attitudes, mental faculties, and viewpoints. We must completely detach ourselves from the evidence of senses and identify with the Omnipotent Healing Presence, paying no attention to appearances and symptoms. Power, faith, confidence, and elevation of consciousness will come as we consider the Divine Masterpiece within and not the appearance

Here is a treatment I use in treating mental disorders such as insanity, etc. I go within myself, mention the name of the patient; then I think of God for three or four minutes by mentally dwelling on Infinite Peace, Harmony, Divine Intelligence, Divine Love, and Wisdom. At the same time I claim that that which is true of God is true of the one I am praying for. I try to get the *feel* that all is order, harmony, bliss, peace, and joy in the mind of the person being prayed for. In this way I induce the mood or mental atmosphere of peace, health, and harmony. When I feel that I have done the best I can, I leave it and pronounce the person whole. I may repeat this treatment two or three times a day or as often as I am led to do so, always praying as if I had never prayed before. If I have only a partial realization, the person in question will feel better. The main thing is to keep on keeping on until the *day breaks and the shadows flee away* in your own mind.

The main purpose of all our prayers for others is to get the feeling of inward joy, and God will do the rest. In prayer we must go to *heaven*; that means a state of inner peace and rest. As we enter this *heaven* frequently, we shall see heaven on earth.

And he was teaching in one of the synagogues on the sabbath. And, behold, there was a woman which had a spirit of infirmity eighteen years, and was bowed together, and could in no wise lift up herself. And when Jesus saw her, he called her to him, and said unto her, Woman, thou art loosed from thine infirmity. And he laid his hands on her: and immediately she was made straight, and glorified God. And the ruler of the synagogue answered with indignation, because that Jesus had healed on the sabbath day, and said unto the people, There are six days in which men ought to work: in them therefore come and be healed, and not on the sabbath day. The Lord then answered him, and said, Thou hypocrite, doth not each one of you on the sabbath loose his ox or his ass from the stall, and lead him away to watering? And ought not this woman, being a daughter of Abraham, whom Satan hath bound, lo, these eighteen years, be loosed from this bond on the sabbath day? Luke 13:10-16,

Healing by the laying on of hands has gone on for countless generations. I have seen some remarkable healings performed in that manner. Some say they are gifted and that their hands are *healing hands.* Of course if they believe that they have this divine gift of healing, it is done unto them as they believe. The truth of the matter is that all of us have the gift of healing. It is not a divine prerogative bestowed on the few. The Healing Presence is operating within you twenty-four hours a day. Did you ever consider all the cuts, bruises, and scratches you experienced when young? Did you not notice an Infinite Intelligence at work? It formed thrombin, closed up the cut, gave you new cells, and a complete healing took place. This happened in all probability without your being aware of it. The Intelligence within is constantly renewing your body. Faith causes this Healing Power to speed up tremendously, so much so that you can experience an instantaneous healing. As a matter of fact, a great number of churches of all denominations practice the laying on of hands.

We are told that the woman in the Bible story was healed on the *sabbath.* Many practice the *sabbath* from a literal standpoint, thinking it is a sin to drive a nail on the sabbath or do work of any kind. Some go to extremes and won't even handle money on the sabbath. All this is meaningless. *The sabbath* is an inner stillness, an inner certitude, whereby man reminds himself of the availability of the God-Presence in all emergencies, at all times, everywhere. You are *walking in the sabbath* when you accept in your mind that your prayer is answered. When you meditate and pray and succeed in reaching the point of inner peace; then your prayer is answered. You have reached the seventh day, the seventh hour, which psychologically means the moment of conviction. You are in the *sabbath* when your heart is aflame with the Glory of God and the certainty of His response, and at that moment you will experience an instantaneous, Divine transfusion of energy, power, vitality, and life.

We must realize that external acts, ritual, ceremony, and conforming to rites, precepts, and ordinances of some organization or church is not real religion or true worship. A man may observe all the rules and regulations of his church and at the same time violate all the laws of God in his heart. He could go to church every day of the week and yet be very unreligious. We must become aware of the fact that the only change that matters is the internal change, the change of the heart, where you have actually fallen in love with spiritual values; then all fear, enemies, and sickness will fall away.

When you walk in the consciousness of peace, health, and happiness, you are *in the sabbath* all day long. You are *in the sabbath* when you feel and know that it is impossible for your prayer to fail. You are unmoved, undisturbed, calm, serene, and tranquil because you are carrying in your subjective mind a divine impression, a subconscious embodiment of your ideal. You know that there is always an interval of time between the subjective embodiment and the objective manifestation. Your inner certitude and imperturbability is the sabbath, and *it was on the sabbath day that she was healed.*

The *ruler of the synagogue* mentioned in the Bible means the ruling thought or prevailing worldly viewpoint or opinion. *The synagogue* is your mind where the aggregation of thoughts, feelings, moods, and opinions gather. Jesus is always available, which means when you are looking at your desire, you are really looking at Jesus, or your solution, or that which saves. *The Woman who has the infirmity* means the feeling of weakness, the depressed state of consciousness, the subjective belief in some crippling disease. The word *woman* means emotional nature, the subjective side of life. Whatever our disease, it represents a negative pattern of thought, charged with emotion in our subliminal depths. The *ruler of the synagogue* represents the fear thoughts, the doubts, and arguments which come to your mind trying to dissuade you to turn away from the belief in the One Power which can do all things. There is an argument in your mind and you must psychologically slay these hypocritical thoughts, by asking them where they come from. Is there a principle behind them? Are they not shadows of the mind? The fear thoughts have no heavenly credentials. Take your attention away from them altogether and they die of neglect. Feast on God's Almighty Power, accept it, imagine that you are being healed now. Do this as often as necessary and you will experience *the sabbath*, or the fullness of acceptance; then you will rise and walk. *It is the sabbath day for you.*

Chapter
5

THE INCURABLE ARE CURED

And it came to pass, as he went into the house of one of the chief Pharisees to eat bread on the sabbath day, that they watched him. And, behold, there was a certain man before him which had the dropsy. And Jesus answering spake unto the lawyers and Pharisees, saying, Is it lawful to heal on the sabbath day? And they held their peace. And he took him, and healed him, and let him go; And answered them, saying, Which of you shall have an ass or an ox fallen into a pit, and will not straightway pull him out on the sabbath day? And they could not answer him again to these things. Luke 14:1-6.

The *Pharisee* is everywhere; he is the type of man who lays stress on external acts and observances. He adheres to the letter of the law and lacks the love and understanding behind the words of the Gospel. The *Pharisee* believes that the fan gives him a stiff neck, that germs are the cause of his cold, and that the hidden virus is the cause of his influenza. The weather, conditions, and circumstances influence the mind in a suggestive way only. Man is the only thinker in his world; therefore it follows that the fan can't give him a cold except he thinks it does. A belief is a thought in the mind generally accepted as true. Many people can sit under a fan all day without getting a cold or a stiff neck. If one accepts the hypnotic suggestion that he will catch cold because of a draft, the fact still remains that the cold was due to his own thought. He had the power to reject or accept the suggestion. If accepted, the

51

result is due to the movement of his own mind. He has no one to blame but himself. His mind accepted a false idea and produced the consequences.

The case of *dropsy* mentioned in the above Gospel story was due to a flood of negativity. When the mind is full of strain, stress, and tension, a corresponding effect is produced in the body, and there is a breakdown in the organs of elimination. If a man is possessed with hatred or deep-seated resentment, it could well bring on an internal flood which, if not checked, could terminate in disintegration of his vital organs due to the corrosive effect of these mental poisons. The conditions in the body are outpicturings of man's mental attitude or states of consciousness.

I knew a man in London who was very religious and completely free from any ill will or resentment. However, he saw his father die of dropsy, and it made a very deep impression on him; he told me that all his life he feared that the same thing would happen to him. He added that his father used to be tapped with an instrument and that the doctor would draw out large amounts of water from his abdominal area. This lingering fear, which was never neutralized, was undoubtedly the cause of his dropsical condition. He did not know the simple psychological truth which Quimby elucidated about a hundred years ago. Quimby said that *if you believed something, it will manifest whether you are consciously thinking of it or not.* This man's fear became a belief that he would become a victim of the same disorder that troubled his father. This explanation helped the man considerably. He began to realize that he had accepted a lie as the truth. The truth began to dawn on him that his fear was a perversion of the truth, a fear which had no real power because there is no principle behind discord. There is a principle of health, none of disease; a principle of abundance, none of poverty; a principle of honesty, none of deceit; a principle of mathematics, none of error; a principle of beauty, none of ugliness. His belief was the only power which controlled him. One's mind can be moved negatively or positively and can be influenced by good or evil.

This man saw the truth about his situation and cast out the lie. He reasoned that the Healing Power which made him was still with him and that his disease was due to a disordered group of thoughts; thus he rearranged his mind to conform to the Divine pattern. Before going to sleep at night he would affirm with feeling and with a deep meaning behind each word, "The Healing Presence is now going to work transforming, healing, restoring, and controlling all processes of my body according to its Wisdom and Divine Nature. I rest secure in this knowledge. I know it is God in action. There is no other power and this Healing Power is working now." He repeated this prayer every night for about thirty days. At the end of that time his mind had reached a conviction of health. This was the *sabbath day* for him, which meant the moment of complete fulfillment in his mind.

I attended a church service some years ago during which the minister gave a very fine talk on Divine Healing. After the service a member of the minister's church board said to him, "It's all right to say, 'Jesus healed', but don't say we can do it Can you imagine a statement like that in this so-called enlightened age? The man who said that had had hundreds of healings all through his life. Life is forever healing our cuts, bruises, sprains, and scratches. It never condemns us. When we take some contaminated food, the same Life-Principle which seeks to preserve us causes us to regurgitate and tries its utmost to heal us. A healing will take place if, as Emerson says, "we take our bloated nothingness out of the way."

I knew a Christian Scientist who swallowed a poisonous liquid by mistake one time. He was a splendid practitioner and had great faith in the God-Power. He told me that he was a hundred miles away from any kind of help so that he had to rely solely on the subjective power within him. He got very still and these are the words he used, "God is in His Holy Temple and His Presence fills every organ and cell of my being. Where God is there is only order, beauty, and perfect functioning. His Holy Presence neutralizes everything unlike itself." He kept this up for an hour and, though in a very weakened condition, had a complete recovery.

Could one take a corrosive poison trusting the subjective power to nullify baneful effects? I don't suggest that anyone take on such a trial. I definitely believe that in an emergency or through a mistaken situation, the sincere truth student looking loyally to God for help could actually prove St. Mark's statement, *And if they drink any deadly thing it shall not hurt them*, and come out unscathed by the experience.

There are mental as well as physical poisons. The lawyers and the Pharisees are in all of us. They represent man-made laws and opinions, and the belief that we are being punished for our sins, that our *karma* is catching up to us, that we have sinned in a former life, and that now we are expiating our sins. Pharisaical thoughts come floating into our mind saying, "We must not question God, maybe it is God's Will that we be sick. This is the cross we must bear." Others have a martyr complex and say, "God is testing me, this is a trial. I must accept my suffering as the Will of God."

God's *Will* is the will of life, and life wants to manifest itself as health, harmony, joy, wholeness, perfection, and abundance. The Will of God is the Nature of God, which is Boundless Love, Infinite Intelligence, Absolute Harmony, Perfect Peace, Infinite Joy, Boundless Wisdom, and Perfect Order, Symmetry, and Proportion. Life cannot wish death. Peace cannot wish pain. Joy cannot wish sorrow. Harmony cannot wish discord. Order cannot wish disorder. Love cannot wish punishment, misery, and suffering. People who say that God is punishing them would never dream of accusing or attributing to their own parents the things of which they accuse God. To such people the words *Infinitely Good* and *Perfect* seem to have no meaning.

Many diseases follow such false beliefs, for all our beliefs tend to manifest themselves. To believe that God is testing you or punishing you sets in motion the law of your own mind bringing trouble, opposition, sickness, and difficulties of all kinds. That is why you hear a man say a jinx is following him. If man has a false premise, his conclusion or experience must conform with his false premise. Actually man punishes himself. He gives everything to himself, whether sorrow or joy, pain or peace.

Jesus means you, yourself, operating your conscious and subconscious mind synchronously and harmoniously. When you know the laws of your mind and apply them constructively, you are the Jesus of the Bible, raising the dead desires, healing the blind thoughts, and walking triumphantly toward your goal. You are no longer blind, halt, withered, or lame. This is why the Bible says, *And he took him, and healed him, and let him go.*

I have outlined for you in this chapter how a man healed a similar condition in himself. The same Healing Power is present in all men. It is not something that only existed two thousand years ago. It is Omnipresent. You can lay hold of it and perform what we call miracles in your life. We must remember that a miracle cannot prove that which is impossible. It is a confirmation of that which is possible, always was, and always will be. For with God all things are possible.

Love, joy, and peace had no beginning and will have no end. Harmony always has been. The Principle of Life always has existed. It is not something that one man possessed. To say this would be the essence of absurdity. Don't wait for some angel or saint to heal you. Don't wonder whether God wants you to be healed or not. Realize that you are violating God's laws which are written in your heart and nature when you are sick, morose, hateful, or poor. Mental poisons are wrong thoughts which work underground in consciousness like a contaminated stream to emerge even after years of wrong experiences such as illness, loss, unhappiness, etc.

The first step in healing is not to be afraid of the manifest conditions from this very moment. The second step is to realize that the condition is but the product of past thinking which will have no more power to continue its existence. The third step is to *exalt the God who is in the midst of thee* (subjective self). This will stop the production of all toxins in you or your patient. You have now pronounced the condition false; in lifting yourself up, seeing the person as he ought to be, you draw the manifestation or the ideal state to you. Live in the embodiment of your desire and the *word* (your thought and feeling) will soon be made flesh. If you allow yourself to be swayed by the beliefs of man (mental poisons), you will not be able to live emotionally in your embodiment.

Among the most deadly mental poisons are the following: Hatred, which is really ignorance, and self-pity, which is really self-absorption. These drugs creep through the psychic bloodstream poisoning all springs of hope and faith, leading to dementia, praecox, melancholia, and other forms of mental derangement. The spiritual antidote is to find your *other* real Self (God) and become God-intoxicated. You can fall madly in love with the new knowledge that thoughts are things and that by filling your mind with spiritual values, you will transform your whole life, bringing you health, happiness, love, and joy. You can fall in love and become wildly enthusiastic in knowing that there is a Principle of Life which flows through your mental patterns and imagery creating after their image and likeness. When you realize that the law of attraction is forever operating in your life, you are seized with a Divine frenzy at the wonder of it all. You are now in love (emotionally attached) with God, or all things good, pleasing, elevating, and uplifting. You now hunger and thirst for more Wisdom and you move forward in the light of the One Who Forever Is.

Old age is another mental poison. The Bible looks upon age *not as the flight of years, but as the dawn of wisdom.* Seek the Divine Frenzy which cleanses you of all toxins. Like Daniel, even in the lions' den, exalt the God within you—the Divine Anti-Body.

Chapter
6

THE HEALING POWER OF THANKSGIVING

And it came to pass, as he went to Jerusalem, that he passed through the midst of Samaria and Galilee. And as he entered into a certain village, there met him ten men that were lepers, which stood afar off: And they lifted up their voices, and said, Jesus, Master, have mercy on us. And when he saw them, he said unto them, Go shew yourselves unto the priests. And it came to pass, that, as they went, they were cleansed. And one of them, when he saw that he was healed, turned back, and with a loud voice glorified God, And fell down on his face at his feet, giving him thanks: and he was a Samaritan. And Jesus answering said, Were there not ten cleansed? But where are the nine? There are not found that returned to give glory to God, save this stranger. And he said unto him, Arise, go thy way: thy faith hath made thee whole. Luke 17:11-19.

This wonderful account of ten lepers being healed is a story of all of us. If you remove the stories of healings in the four Gospels, you have certainly emasculated one of the most important parts of the Gospels. The story of the lepers is telling all of us that sickness of the body has its origin in sickness of the soul.

I remember reading some time ago a report of a statement made by Dr. Elmer Hess as he was inaugurated president of the American Medical Association to the effect that a physician who does not believe in God has no business in a sick room. I believe that most physicians agree that faith in God has a profound effect in the maintenance of perfect health. Let us remind ourselves at this point of the famous saying, "The doctor treats the patient; God heals him."

As previously pointed out, the word *leper* in the Bible means a mind troubled with conflicting desires, emotions, and confused ideas. It means a sick mind, a man who is sick in his thoughts, his emotions, and his body. Leprosy is a wasting disease; therefore it typifies the state of a man who has lost his vitality, energy, enthusiasm, and vigor for life, because he has psychologically separated himself from the Source of all life. We have a leprous condition when we are full of envy, jealousy, anger, hatred, self-condemnation, etc.

When the Bible says *Jesus passed through Samaria and Galilee to reach Jerusalem,* it refers to a process of prayer or steps of prayer. *Jesus* represents the ideal, your desire, plan, or purpose which is always walking down the streets of your mind beckoning you onward and upward. Your ideal, picture, or vision is at this moment saying to you, "Rise up and accept me." When you raise your desire up in consciousness to the point of acceptance, you experience the truth of the statement, *Thy faith hath made thee whole.* Your desire must go through *Samaria,* which means confusion, double-mindedness, and conflict *in Galilee* (your mind).

The numeral *ten* mentioned here symbolizes the completion of a process. To look at it in a very simple way, the numeral *one* means the male or pressing aspect, namely your idea or desire. The naught or circle symbolizes a womb or receptive mind of man. *Woman* means the *womb of man.* In other words, *ten* means the interaction of the male and female elements of your own mind, thought and feeling, idea and emotion, the brain and heart. When these two are functioning harmoniously, constructively, and joyously, it is a happy marriage or union. Such a person is well integrated, healthy, vital, and courageous. The thoughts must be united with true feeling. Our thoughts must conform to the spiritual standard set forth by Paul, *Whatsoever things are true, whatsoever things are honest, whatsoever things are just, whatsoever things are pure, whatsoever things are lovely, whatsoever things are of good report; if there be any virtue, and if there be any praise, think on these things.* Phil. 4:8.

True emotion follows true thought. The heart or subjective feeling nature should be the chalice of God's Love as it is the sanctuary of His Holy Presence. It is called the *cup* in the Bible. As we meditate on the spiritual values of life we receive a transfusion of love, faith, confidence, and energy which courses through our veins transforming our whole being. Our faith is kindled when we realize that all things are done by faith, which is a movement of Omnipotence within ourselves. There is only one power and that is our own consciousness. When we think of something, we have at that moment pin-pointed the flow of the Almighty Creative Power through one focal point of attention. Our faith is really our thought which, as Baudouin the French psychologist said, begins to execute itself immediately, taking form and function in your life.

All of us want to go to *Jerusalem*, the city of peace within ourselves, which means that when our desire is completely subjectified, we have reached the place of accomplishment or fulfillment. We are now at peace (Jerusalem). Our mind is no longer divided. The two (desire and faith) have become one and all is well.

The number *ten* is also a sacred number and bears reference to the line 1, and the circle 0, which produce a cross (X) only when there is a conflict in the mind. This conflict and frustration follows when man is in a double minded state. He has two powers and believes in good and evil. He looks at his environment, circumstances, and conditions and says to himself, "It's hopeless, all is lost, there is no way out of this dilemma, I'm incurable," and many similar statements. He is transferring the power within himself to external conditions, perhaps he is blaming the weather, other people, or a jinx for his trouble.

When desire and fear quarrel, the mind and the body become a battleground resulting in wasteful expenditures of energy, debility of the vital organs, nervous prostration, and exhaustion.

Man must learn not to make a created thing or the manifested world a cause. He must not exalt the created thing above the Creator. He must resolve the conflict by going within himself and, like Quimby, placing his case before the Great Tribunal, God, the only Presence and the only Power. In the secret chamber of his own mind, he gives supreme recognition to the Spirit within. He looks at the fearful, negative thoughts and orders them out of his mind, realizing that they are only an illusion of power. There is no principle behind them and there is nothing to sustain them. He reminds himself that there is only one Creative Power and that it is now flowing through his thought-patterns bringing him the good he seeks. He keeps on doing this regularly and systematically until a healing of the situation takes place. He has reached a decision or pronounced judgment in his own mind. He has condemned the guilty cause (the negative thoughts) and has freed his prisoner (desire) into the arms of the Lord (his subjective self), where, through repetition, faith, and expectancy, his desire has sunk deeply into his subconscious mind. This is called depth therapy or as the Bible calls it, entering Jerusalem (uru—city, salem—peace), i.e., reaching the point of conviction.

The cross we have been carrying is now removed because we have reached the place of death. Our desire has been entombed where it dies first; then comes forth as the answer to our prayer. The word (thought) has become flesh (made manifest in our body and environment).

The cry of the ten lepers is the cry of every man. It is the appeal of every troubled, frustrated, and neurotic person to the Master or Spiritual Power within, which alone can give peace and health of mind, body, and emotions. They lifted up their voices. You lift yourself up mentally when you turn in reverence, allegiance, and adoration to the Spiritual Presence within who healeth all thy diseases. Master, have mercy on us. The hundredth Psalm says, His mercy is everlasting. How beautiful are these words. They touch the heart strings causing you to go forth with the praise of God forever on your lips.

Go skew yourselves unto the priests. The word priest is a symbol of spiritual perception, an intuitive awareness of the great Truths of God. A priest is one who offers up a sacrifice. Every man is a priest of God when he turns away from the false gods and the poisoned feast of the irrational, mass-mind with its fears, superstitions, and terrors in order to give his supreme attention to the one God and His Laws. He sacrifices or gives up his negative thoughts, fears, and false beliefs and contemplates love, peace, beauty, and perfection. He must give to receive. He gives up, i.e., fasts from resentment and feasts on love; fasts from the idea of poverty and feasts on the idea of God's abundance; fasts from fear and feasts on faith in God and all things good; fasts from sadness and secretes the essence of joy, knowing that the joy of the Lord is his strength. The true priest fasts from pain and feasts on God's Silent River of Peace. He fasts from self-condemnation, depression, and self-pity, and feasts on amiability, sociability, kindliness, good will, and laughter. He fasts from symptoms and feasts on the mental vision of health and happiness. He fasts from darkness and feasts on the Light of God being reflected on all his problems, knowing the Light (intelligence) of God knows only the answer. He fasts from karma, fate, predestination, and feasts on God, the Eternal Now, knowing the Absolute does not condemn, judge, punish, or send sickness, disease, or death. He knows that though his hands are dripping with the blood of others and though he may have committed dastardly crimes, he can instantaneously turn to the Presence of God within, lifting himself up to the Heart of God, claiming and feeling that he now is the man God intended him to be, the happy man, the joyous man, the poised man, the peaceful man, the loving man. As this man paints a picture or vision in his mind and his heart, he hungers for an inward change; the Law of God automatically responds to his new mental pattern, and the past is forgotten and remembered no more.

If man misused the laws of chemistry or electricity for twenty years, the moment he used the principle correctly the underlying laws of chemistry or electricity would automatically respond. The law cannot possibly hold grudges or try to get even. When we are dealing with our mind, we are also using the principle of mind. It makes no difference if you have been a murderer, a thief, or if you have committed all manner of evil, the moment you decide sincerely to change your life by enthroning a new concept and estimate of yourself in your mind and feel the truth of that which you affirm, the law reverses its former action and responds by corresponding to the new blueprint of your mind.

We must realize that the perfunctory prayer will not suffice. Only when sincerity and a new spiritual view of things takes hold of the mind do you expunge from your deeper mind the former negative patterns which caused all your trouble. You must remember that the law plays no favorites; moreover law is always impersonal. The laws of our mind never punish us. We merely experience the reaction of the law which we set in motion by our thoughts and beliefs. When man understands this, he has no occasion to hate or resent the meanest man who walks the earth. Furthermore, there is no basis for ill will, resentment, envy, or jealousy for all men may turn within for what they want. As they positively assert this claim for the good they seek, the law of mind responds to their mental acceptance.

There is no basis for harboring ill feeling toward people who defraud or cheat us. There is nothing lost unless we admit the loss in our mind. All we have to do is to realize that all things exist in Infinite Mind, identify ourselves mentally and emotionally with that which we want, and our exchequer will again be replenished from the Infinite reservoir of God's riches in ways we know not of. There is no loss but the sense of loss. People who rob, defraud, or otherwise deceive us are merely messengers telling us who we have conceived ourselves to be. They testify to our state of consciousness. How could we be angry or hostile to others when they are merely instruments of our own mind, fulfilling the play which we wrote consciously or unconsciously in the book of life, our subconscious mind. It is easy to forgive; all we have to do is to forgive ourselves for having negative, destructive thoughts which hurt us, while those with whom we were angry probably have been fishing, dancing, or having a glorious time.

To heal any situation, *you show yourself to the priest*, for you are the *priest* yourself, forever giving up the lesser for the greater. You may offer your *sacrifice* now, which is your desire for a perfect healing, by directing your attention from the symptoms and the body, and dwelling with the Lord of Life within. Claim that the Infinite Healing Presence is saturating every atom of your body, making you whole, pure, and perfect. Know and feel that the Living Intelligence which made your body is now taking over, causing all the organs of your body to conform to God's eternal pattern of harmony, health, and peace. As you enter into the mental atmosphere of harmony, health, and peace, a rearrangement of your thought-patterns takes place followed automatically by molecular changes in the body structure to conform to the new state of consciousness. You are now transformed because you have had a spiritual transfusion of the Healing Power released by your prayers so that every atom of your being dances to the rhythm of the Eternal God.

Were there not ten cleansed? But where are the nine? The numeral *nine* mentioned refers to the consciousness of possession. Possession is nine points of the law when we enter into the feeling of being what we long to be, or as we continue to claim and feel as true that which we affirm; we add thought to thought, mood to mood, and finally we reach the point of fulfillment in consciousness. The next step is *ten*, or our good made manifest. The cycle of consciousness has been completed; we are back where we started. We began thinking of God (the One), and we ended experiencing God (the One). Everything resolves itself back to ONE, its starting point. You glorify God each time your prayer is answered. Your thought and feeling become one as they are fused together by enthusiasm and love. The *issue* is the son in expression, the idea objectified.

It is said the one who gave thanks was a *stranger*. The *stranger* in your mind might be sickness, fear, worry, or a business difficulty.

These negative attitudes are *strangers*, aliens in the house of God. Our mind is supposed to be a house of prayer, not a den of thieves. Fear, worry, and anger are the *strangers* and intruders who rob us of peace of mind. When we starve these states through neglect, by giving all our attention and devotion to God and His Attributes and Qualities, our mind is cleansed. At that moment we are praising and exalting the God in the midst of us.

And one of them, when he saw that he was healed, turned back, and with a loud voice glorified God, And fell down on his face at his feet, giving him thanks. Here is a perfect formula of prayer. You may be expressing yourself in a wonderful way, be happily married, have a very prosperous business, have wonderful friends, yet, you may have a bad heart or have trouble with your eyes.

There was a man in our recent class on the *Book of Job* who wrote me saying that he was leaving the nine harmonious, stable conditions of his life to fill up the one that was lost or missing. He said that he went to work on a quality in which he was sadly lacking, namely, thankfulness. This young man said he rarely praised anybody and that he was not thankful for all his blessings. He was amazed when he began to consider all the wonderful things that happened to him and the many blessings he enjoyed. The *stranger* in his midst was eye trouble. The mood of gratitude and the thankful heart causes us to tune in with the creative forces of the universe and what we send out comes back to us multiplied by the law of action and reaction. This young man quieted the wheels of his mind and began to imagine he was talking to the King of Kings, the Lord of Lords within himself. He had no mental picture of God, of course. In his mind's eye he sensed that the Divine Presence was there, the very Life of him. He began to say, over and over again, "Thank you Father, Thank you Father." He kept repeating this softly, quietly, gently, and lovingly. He was in a sleepy, drowsy, state each night as he meditated in the manner outlined. He would go to sleep in the mental mood of thankfulness. He had a perfect healing of his eyes. In biblical language *he fell down on his face at his feet.* The word *face* means the

Truth and Presence of God; *feet* mean understanding. *To fall down is* to humble yourself and set aside the intellect, knowing that Infinite Wisdom and Power are within and can do all things. He understood that vision is spiritual, eternal, and indestructible, and that all he had to do was to enter into the mood of thankfulness for the gift already received. The grateful heart is the mind which believes and rejoices in the joy of the answered prayer. You have oftentimes thanked the man behind the counter for the coat, wrap, or suit which you paid for, but did not receive. You know that he will send it to you and you trust him implicitly. God's promises never fail and you can also give thanks for the gifts which have already been given you. Rise to the point of acceptance and go forth with a grateful heart for the gift already received.

I have been a stranger in a strange land. Ex. 2:22. All of us are really wanderers, pilgrims, and strangers here. We have left Paradise and do not feel at home here. Our pilgrimage is back to the One. We have loves, urges, ideals, and aspirations; and as we look at the world, it seems to deny the inner whisperings and murmurings of our heart strings which remind us of our origin and urge us back to it.

There is only one thing to do; there is only one thing all men are seeking, and that is the God within, the Creative Presence and Power. Leave the good, sound qualities, aspects, conditions, and circumstances of your life and find the *stranger,* the thing that bothers you, that is at present annoying you. Some desire perhaps is not fulfilled. Turn to God within and still the wheels of your mind; immobilize your attention, focus your mental lens on the fact that the Spirit within you, God, is the Cause and the Source of all your good. Then give thanks by silently repeating, "Thank you," over and over again as a lullaby, until your mind is full of the feeling of thankfulness. Continue to do this until you are filled in consciousness. The moment you qualify or condition your consciousness, the answer will come. The *lepers* are now cleansed. Let your prayer be "O God, give me one more thing, a grateful heart."

Chapter

7

EYESIGHT RESTORED

And it came to pass, that as he was come nigh unto Jericho, a certain blind man sat by the way side begging: And hearing the multitude pass by, he asked what it meant. And they told him, that Jesus of Nazareth passeth by. And he cried, saying, Jesus, Thou son of David, have mercy on me. And Jesus stood, and commanded him to be brought unto him: and when he was come near, he asked him, Saying, What wilt thou that 1 shall do unto thee? And he said, Lord, that 1 may receive my sight. And Jesus said unto him, Receive thy sight: thy faith bath saved thee. And immediately he received his sight, and followed him, glorifying God: and all the people, when they saw it, gave praise unto God. Luke 18:35-43. Related passages, Mark 10:46-52.

There is the well known, duly authenticated case of Madame Bire. She was blind, the optic nerves were atrophied, useless. She visited Lourdes and had what she termed a miraculous healing. Ruth Cranston, a Protestant young lady who investigated and wrote about healings at Lourdes in *McCall's Magazine*, November, 1955, writes about Madame Bire as follows: "At Lourdes she regained her sight, incredibly, with the optic nerves still lifeless and useless, as several doctors could testify after repeated examinations. A month later, upon re-examination, it was found that the seeing mechanism had been restored to normal. But at first, so far as medical examination could tell, she was seeing with 'dead eyes'."

I visited Lourdes in 1955 where I, too, witnessed some

healings, and of course there is no doubt but that healings take place at various shrines throughout the world, Christian and Non-Christian.

Madame Bire, to whom we just referred, was not healed by the waters or by the Shrine, but by her belief. The healing principle within herself responded to the nature of her thought. Belief is a thought in the mind. It means to accept something as true. The thought accepted executes itself automatically. Faith means to accept that what you are praying for already is. Undoubtedly Madame Bire went to the Shrine with expectancy and great faith, knowing in her heart she would receive a healing. Her deeper mind responded to her belief and Spiritual forces were released, restoring her vision according to her belief. *According to your belief is it done unto you.* The Healing Presence which created the eyes can certainly bring a dead nerve back to life. What the Creative Principle Created in the first place, it can recreate.

Healings occur sometimes unheralded at various religious services. Some people have told me that they had healings at our healing service on Sunday mornings. They add that they did not expect a healing, that they were skeptical, that they were in no state of exaltation, and were not even thinking of a healing. From what they say one would gather that they lacked faith; therefore the question arises, how could they receive a healing? The answer is rather simple. They are looking for a healing and their minds are open and receptive to receive the prayers of the multitude present. Perhaps they are going to a doctor, osteopath, or chiropractor for treatment, which is highly indicative that they desire to be healed. Desire is prayer; this attitude indicates a very receptive mind for the idea of perfect health to be resurrected, for which the people present are praying. When a group of people, gathered together in prayer, affirm that all those who are present are healed, made whole and perfect, they are establishing a definite psychological and spiritual link among all those present; then even if unbelievers or skeptics are present, it is possible for them to be healed for the simple reason that they desire a healing.

You might ask the question, "What about a person who is full of hatred, ill will, and resentment, would he get a healing at a Shrine or at any church healing service?" If the faucet or a pipeline is full of debris of all sorts, the water will not flow freely; furthermore, the water will be muddy and contaminated. It is necessary to remove the kinks in the hose when watering the garden. Your body is the garden, and when you pray you are watering your garden with the Healing Power of God. The healing waters are love, peace, joy, faith, good will, confidence, and strength. The man full of hate is opposed to the stream of love and joy. He must decide to let go of his grudges and pet peeves, and to let in the sunshine of God's Love. His mental block sets up a resistance to the Healing Principle and a short circuit takes place. When he lets down the bars, the invasion of love and grace can penetrate. A person who refuses to resolve his mental conflicts definitely delays his healing. The consciousness of love is the most potent healing force in the world. The doctor, priest, rabbi, or New Thought minister possessing the greatest measure of God's Love will get the best results.

Jesus said to the blind man, *What wilt thou that I shall do unto thee? And he said, Lord, that I may receive my sight.* The beggar was specific because he knew what he wanted and said so. Life is always asking you, *what wilt thou of me?* What is your desire? Millions of people are blind; i.e., they are psychologically and spiritually blind because they do not know that they become what they think all day long. Man is spiritually blind when he hates, resents, or is envious of others. He does not know that he is actually secreting mental poisons which tend to destroy him.

Thousands of people are constantly saying that there is no way to solve their problems, that the situation is hopeless. Such an attitude is the result of spiritual blindness. Man begins to see spiritually and mentally when he gets a new perception of the mind, knowing that there is an Infinite Intelligence within him that is responsive to his thought which can solve all problems. The cry of the world is, "I want my sight." Men, women, and children should receive their sight. They should be taught in schools, in colleges, and in homes throughout the land, where the Creative Principle of Life is and how to use it. They should be taught the interrelationship of the conscious and subconscious mind.

Emerson said, "A man is what he thinks all day long." The Bible says, *As a man thinketh in his heart so is he.* Men should be taught that the Principle of Life is responsive to their thought and that when they claim that Infinite Intelligence leads and guides them, revealing to them the perfect answer, they find themselves automatically led to do the right thing as the way opens up. They were once *blind* to these truths; they now begin to *see* the vision of health, wealth, and happiness, and peace of mind.

And Jesus said unto him, Receive thy sight: thy faith hath saved thee. Jesus symbolizes the Redeemer or the Healing Principle of Life within all of us which forever responds to our expectancy or faith. Your faith is your feeling, your awareness, your inner conviction that what you are praying for already is. Vision is eternal, spiritual, and indestructible. We do not create vision, we manifest or release it.

Recently a woman came to me with incipient glaucoma, which is hardening of the eyeball. I read some time ago an article which stated that ophthalmologists in one of the larger hospitals discovered that there was a pattern of hatred in about twenty to twenty-five percent of the cases of glaucoma in the hospital. This is not true in all cases, of course. In others who indulge in negative or destructive thinking, the liver, heart, lungs, or other organs may be affected, depending on the susceptibility of the person. The disease may also be due to fear, or race mind impinging on the consciousness of people who fail to pray. This woman began to pray for a daughter-in-law whom she hated intensely. She did it this way: "I release unto God. I wish for her all of God's happiness, peace, and joy." She repeated this prayer frequently until all the roots were withered in her mind. Actually she began to feel kindly toward the daughter-in-law after a few weeks. This is how true love melts everything unlike itself. We prayed together frequently; we were *en rapport* with each other. All of us are sending and receiving stations. She was open and receptive to the truth, and she prayed frequently using the prayer "Perfect Eyesight" in one of my books of meditations which is as follows:

"My eyes are God's eyes, and I see perfectly. The Living Intelligence which made my eyes is now controlling the processes and functioning of my eyes and my entire body. I know and believe that my vision is spiritual, eternal, and indestructible. "If, therefore thine eye be single, thy whole body shall be full of light." This means I see only the Truth; I love the Truth; I know the Truth. I see God in all men and in all things. I see spiritually, mentally, and physically. My eyes reflect the glory, the beauty, and the perfection of God. It is God looking out through my eyes seeing His own ideas of perfection. My eyes are the windows of my soul; they are pure, and are kept single to Love, Truth, and Beauty at all times. The harmonizing, healing, vitalizing, energizing Power of the Holy Spirit permeates every atom, cell, nerve, tissue, and muscle of my eyes making them whole, pure, and perfect. The Divine, perfect pattern is now made manifest in my eyes, and every atom and cell conforms to God's perfect pattern on the Mount. Thank you, Father."

She let these truths sink down by a process of spiritual osmosis into her deeper mind and gradually a perfect healing took place. She cooperated perfectly with her doctor, praying for him also. At the end of a few months, she had no longer any occasion for the eye drops. The doctor said all tension had disappeared.

I know many people who have had miraculous results with the following simple prayer. "I see spiritually; I see mentally; I see physically; It is wonderful." They fill their soul (subjective nature) with the sense of wonder, and wonders happen when they pray. Jesus, Moses, Elijah, and Paul could not use any other Healing Principle than the one you are using. It is the same yesterday, today, and forever.

When our thought-patterns are disorganized, we are sick. Our dark, dismal thoughts hide the vision of our God. When we pray by identifying ourselves with the eternal, spiritual values, a rearrangement of our thought-patterns takes place followed by a molecular change in the body which conforms with the changed mental attitude. The healing follows. Sight is displayed, not created.

If deaf, we hear again the sound of He Who Is. We realize it is God hearing His own sound through His own ears. It is God seeing His own perfect ideas through His own eyes. The woman who was healed of glaucoma had faith and knowledge; she will, of course, have no return of the disease. The healing will be permanent.

A blind faith will bring a healing, but oft times it is impermanent and fallible. Keep your mind fixed on God and His Perfection and your healing powers will be more proficient and successful. As you walk the earth in quiet moments with God, you will be practicing His Presence and releasing His Healing Power all the time without even knowing it.

Remember we see *through* the eye, not with it. The cornea of the eye receives vibrations from objects in space; through the optic nerve these vibrations are carried to the brain. When the inner light or intelligence meets the outer light, we see. "We see because the Seer is within." We see because Infinite Intelligence is the light of our consciousness. If your eyes are not functioning perfectly, the Creative Principle which made them hasn't been hurt or injured. He that made your eyes can also recreate, refashion, and heal them. *Behold, I make all things new.* Your eyes symbolize Divine Love, a delight in the ways of God, and a hunger and thirst for God's Truth. You will always have good vision if you tune in to the Love of He Who Is. The *right eye* symbolizes right thought and right action. The *left eye* symbolizes God's Love and His Wisdom. Think right, radiate good will, and you will focus perfectly.

You can receive your sight. Yes, you can perceive the answer to any problem, be it what it may, by recognizing the Source of all good. Give supreme allegiance to the God-Presence within and feel the reality of what you are praying for. You don't go to God with a problem. You come to God giving thanks for the answer which is yours now as you open your mind to receive.

Receive thy sight. And immediately he received his sight, and followed him, glorifying God.

Chapter

8

HEARING RESTORED

And one of them smote the servant of the high priest, and cut off his right ear. And Jesus answered and said, Suffer ye thus far. And he touched his ear, and healed him. Luke 22:50-51. Many people ask me whether it is right to pray for someone who is sick, troubled, or in some difficulty. Then they usually say, "He didn't ask me to pray for him." As you read the above verses, you are not told that the servant asked Jesus to restore his ear. Jesus apparently didn't wait for the question, but voluntarily restored the ear. It seems like begging the question to ask, "Should I pray for someone in trouble?" Of course you may pray for anyone you wish, and it would be most excellent to pray once a day for all men throughout the world, wishing them harmony, health, peace, and joy. Pray for the President, the Congress, people in your office, your home, and the whole world will be blessed because you have performed such unselfish devotions.

Sometimes I am asked this question, "Should I pray for my mother who does not believe in Divine Healing and is opposed to this teaching about mental and spiritual laws?" The answer is simple. If the mother, father, or relative has no faith in your religious convictions or in your particular technique or process of prayer, that does not make any difference whatever. When you pray for someone, you must not bother with the question of whether he believes or disbelieves, whether he accepts or rejects. Neither do you concern yourself with his church affiliations or his agnosticism; furthermore you pay no attention to his symptoms, aberrations, mental conflicts, or blocks of any kind. You simply enter into the silence of your soul, immobilize your attention, and mentally reject all sense-evidence. You do this decisively and categorically. Quietly know that the Infinite Healing Power is timeless and spaceless and that it embraces the one you are praying for; then you silently feel or quietly affirm the Truth, just as you like. You don't have to use any words. You can *feel* the Truth of what you think, that the Harmony, Health, Power, Peace, Order, and Perfection of God are now being manifested in your friend's mind and body. Know that there is but one mind, and in mind there is neither time nor space. You are one with your friend, because you are thinking of him. In the language of Troward, you are *en rapport* with him, and in the language of Quimby, you are one with him, because our minds mingle like atmospheres and each has his identity in that atmosphere. What you feel and know as true about your friend will be resurrected in his experience. You have taken his request, or his desire for health, and made it your own.

As you contemplate the qualities and attributes of God, knowing that these qualities are now being experienced by your friend, there is an immediate response in the mental structure of your friend, and a reordering of his mind takes place bringing about a perfect healing. Your inner sense of peace and confidence that the law of health and harmony is now in operation brings about a sense of faith and trust in you. As you continue to pray, perhaps two or three times a day, the time will come when you will lose all desire to pray because your prayer is answered. You can't desire what you have. A doctor does not treat a patient who is healed; the patient requires no further treatment. Prayer operates on the same principle. You pray until you need no longer pray.

We see and hear with the mind. In biblical language *we cut off an ear* when we cease listening to the troubled voice of the world with its false beliefs, terrors, and superstitions. *Jesus touching the ear and healing it* means that we should hear the voice of Truth which says, *I am God and there is no God beside me.* We should hear only that which fills our soul with joy. Hear the good news about the other. To what are you giving attention? If you are listening to gossip, criticism, and condemnation, you are not hearing the Truth. If someone tells you that you are going to fail in your enterprise and if you give him any attention, you are not hearing the gospel or good news about yourself.

Go within yourself, place all your attention on the idea of success. You will immediately begin to enter into a mood or feeling of success. You are now hearing the good news because you are under a good spell. You are now absorbed, engrossed, and fascinated by the idea of success, achievement, and accomplishment. You know that fear and success are simply two ideas in the mind. You know that you were born to succeed, and that you have all the equipment necessary. The fear-thought is false, it's an illusion, it's a shadow of the mind. A shadow has no power or substance. The idea of success is real and your subconscious powers will move on your behalf, compelling you to take all the steps necessary, as you give your attention to the idea of success. You are now hearing the Truth.

It is always right to bless the other. Surely there can't be anything wrong with wishing for the other person health, harmony, joy, peace, and all of God's riches. That is the answer to those who say, "Is it wrong to pray for the other if he didn't ask me?" Of course not. You should wish for everyone what you wish for yourself. Love is the fulfilling of the law. Love is sincerely radiating the sunshine of God's Love, Light, and Truth to all men everywhere. This is the Law which brings fulfillment, happiness, peace, and abundance into your own life. What we withhold from another, we withhold from ourselves. Actually there is no other, all of us are in the One Mind and the One Spirit which is Indivisible. There can be no divisions or quarrels in it. One part can't be antagonistic to another part. If that were so there would be no harmony, only chaos. The Infinite cannot be divided.

For example, if you are praying for prosperity and you are resenting the wealth and riches of another, you are condemning what you are praying for, and your good takes wings and flies away. How can you attract wealth when you resent its manifestation in another. You are thinking and feeling lack instead of abundance, and as you think and feel, so are you. Thinking makes consciousness, and your state of consciousness governs your world. When you see this Truth, you are *Jesus,* (illumined reason, awareness of truth) *touching the ear,* (hearing the truth which frees you) and *healing it,* i.e., bringing about a state of wholeness or unity in your mind.

You are told that *he cut off his right ear.* The *right* means the objective world, worldly opinion, sense evidence, and judging according to appearances. *Cut off that right ear now,* once and for all, and give no power to external phenomena. Do not worship or give power to germs, nor bow down in fear before them. Don't get panic-stricken when someone sneezes and say, "Oh, I'll catch a cold." Reject the false belief that a fan will give you a stiff neck, or that the cold night air will give you pneumonia or cause bronchial trouble. The weather has no power over you. We give power to these things because we believe that they affect us; we suffer according to our belief. The fan is harmless, it never said to anyone, "I will give you a cold if you sit near me or under me." The fan is neutral. It is a metallic substance, composed of molecules revolving at a high speed. Bless the fan, bless the weather; God pronounced all things good. When your feet get wet, don't say that the water will give you pneumonia. The water never said that, why do you say it? Man has created countless false gods; and all his trouble arises out of his darkened mind and distorted imagination.

Nicoll of England says that all man's evil is due to misunderstanding. Man sees *through a glass darkly,* due to the twilight in his mind. When the shadows fall in the evening, sometimes man mistakes a stump of a tree with some branches for an enemy with a gun aimed at his heart. He becomes frozen with fear. This is the twilight in his mind. He has not heard, he has not seen. Become Jesus; i.e., become awakened to the Truth and know that there is but one Primal Cause which is your own Consciousness; cease making secondary Causes. To know that your I AM is the only Power, the only Cause, the only Substance, is to free you from all the false gods of the world, enabling you to go forth with the song of God in your heart.

Your *ears* are symbolic of understanding. Many people who complained of their inability to hear the writer at his public lectures on Sunday now sit at the rear of the lecture hall and hear perfectly. Their interest in Truth was aroused; their attention was quickened; and there was a normal, healthy response from the deeper mind. The following is a simple prayer which I give to people suffering from ear troubles of any kind: "I hear the Truth; I love the Truth; I know the Truth. My ears are God's perfect ideas functioning perfectly at all times. My ears are the perfect instruments which reveal God's harmony to me. The Love, Beauty, and Harmony of God flow through my ears; I am in tune with the Infinite. I hear the Still, Small, Voice of God within me. The Healing Presence quickens my hearing and my ears are open and free." My experiences with people have convinced me that a great number of people become deaf, or partially so, because they don't want to hear the voice of someone. They are trying to shut out certain things. If a man has a nagging wife, he may not want to hear her, and gradually he loses his hearing capacity. These negative auto-suggestions sink into his subconscious mind, and the latter proceeds to follow out the suggestion given. You can place man in a trance state and suggest to him that he can't hear until you tell him he can. The subconscious, being amenable to suggestion, accepts the suggestion of the operator and he can't hear; this shows us how our mind works. We must, therefore, be exceedingly careful of the thoughts we entertain and give attention to in our mind.

There are many people who deliberately shut out the Truth. They say, "I don't want to hear a word of that. Shut that man off, I don't want to hear his voice. I hate that voice. I don't want to hear it. I won't hear it," etc. These and similar statements are expressed with such emphasis and feeling that they become highly destructive. Our subconscious mind accepts these statements as requests, and proceeds to bring them to pass in our experience. You have heard the old maxim which contains a great Truth, "There are none so deaf as those that will not hear."

Dr. Flanders Dunbar, famous authority on psychosomatic medicine, cites many cases where deafness was due to mental and emotional disturbances. In her book *Emotions and Bodily Changes*, she cites a case of a man of forty-five who had been married for twenty years and had to use a hearing aid. He ascribed his deafness to swimming. He thought that one advantage of being deaf was that he didn't have to listen to his wife. The doctor asked to examine the hearing aid, but went right on talking. They became engaged in such an animated conversation that it was not until half an hour later that he discovered the doctor was still holding his hearing aid. By now, of course, you have deduced what was wrong with his hearing. His subconscious mind responded to his desire not to listen to his wife. There are people who have a form of deafness due to the fact that their mind is closed to all ideas but their own. They are unyielding, inflexible, dogmatic, and full of pride.

Hearing is a mental and spiritual process. Trust the Divine Intelligence which made your ears and all their parts. *I will restore health unto thee and heal thee of thy wounds with the Lord.*

Chapter
9

PRAYER WIPES OUT ALL KARMA

We have finished with the miracles of healing reported in the book of *Luke*, which have parallel accounts in *Mark* and *Matthew*. The book of *John* is the most mystical book in the Bible. In the ninth chapter of *John*, a story is told of a man *which was blind from his birth.*

And as Jesus passed by, he saw a man which was blind from his birth. And his disciples asked him, saying, Master, who did sin, this man, or his parents, that he was born blind? Jesus answered, Neither hath this man sinned, nor his parents: but that the works of God should be made manifest in him. I must work the works of him that sent me, while it is day: the night cometh, when no man can work. As long as I am in the world I am the light of the world. When he had thus spoken, he spat on the ground, and made clay of the spittle, and he anointed the eyes of the blind man with the clay, And said unto him, Go, wash in the pool of Siloam, (which is by interpretation, Sent.) He went his way therefore, and washed, and came seeing. The neighbors therefore, and they which before had seen him that he was blind, said, Is not this he that sat and begged? Some said, This is he: others said, He is like him: but he said, I am he. John 9:1-9. *Related passages,* Matt. 9:27-30, 12:22, 20:30-34; Mark 10:46-52.

You can read a more extensive account in my books, *The Meaning of Reincarnation*, and *Peace Within Yourself* which gives the psychological meaning of the book of *John*.

In ancient times it was believed that if a man were born blind, it was due to past *karma*, and that he was here to expiate for his sins. The people of that day also believed that the sins of the parents were communicated to the children. For example, if the parents were insane, all their children would be insane.

The *sin* spoken of in the Bible refers to the mental attitude, the mood, the feeling of the parents. All sin refers to movements of the mind rather than that of the body. Parents transmit their habitual thinking, fears, tensions, and false beliefs through the mind, not the body. Our feelings and moods create. What tone do you strike during the marital, creative act?*

There are blind and deaf states of consciousness from which blind and deaf children come forth. Whatever tone is struck by the parents, a corresponding expression comes forth by the laws of reciprocal relationship. There is no instance in the Bible in which anyone was ever refused a healing. The Absolute cannot and does not judge or condemn. All judgment is given to the son, i.e., all judgment is pronounced in your own mind. Each man arrives at his own decision or conclusion, and there is an automatic response of the law. If man thinks negatively, the response is negative. If he thinks positively and constructively, the reaction of the law of his mind is good and very good.

The laws of nature and our mind cannot hold a grudge against us. There is not one law for a child and another for a man of ninety. The moment man goes within himself, claims his good, and presses his claim with faith and confidence, there is the automatic response of the law which honors the mental acceptance of his good. The past is forgotten and remembered no more.

Reason rejects the popular, superstitious belief of the people that man's blindness is due to his *karma*, that he may have blinded people in a former life and is now back on this plane to suffer and atone for his crime. Another very popular, superstitious belief was, and still is, that a child may be born blind because his parents were blind, or because they had sinned or had some physical disease.

---

* See Chapter 4 in my book *The Meaning of Reincarnation.*

A man and wife though congenially blind or blinded by accident may give birth to children with perfectly normal vision.

A mother through prayer, may change the mental and physical nature of her child while he is still in the womb, and bring about a perfect healing. In God's eyes there are no blind, deaf, halt, or lame people. God sees everyone perfect, and His Creation as Infinite Perfection.

I must work the works of him that sent me, while it is day. This means while the Light of Truth is shining, we consciously direct the law.

To make clay of the spittle represents a drooling state, like a boy hungers for candy and drools at the mouth. It represents a joyful, bubbling up state. You have seen geysers bubbling up which make clay look very much alive. The *clay* in the natural state represents the average man who is dead and unaware of the Healing Principle within him. He is, in other words, dead to his inner potentialities. As he awakens and becomes enthusiastic about the discovery of the powers within, he becomes alive to God; this is the meaning of *he spat on the ground and made clay of the spittle.* This latter phrase is an oriental, idiomatic, figurative expression meaning a deep, inner conviction that we now have the consciousness of what we want, and that we reject blindness or the old state of limitation.

We are not here to suffer or expiate for sins or errors. We are here to awaken to the Truth about ourselves and realize that *Beloved, now are we the sons of God,* that *Now is the day of salvation,* and *the Kingdom of Heaven is at hand.* Like Paul you can be changed in the twinkling of an eye.

Remember what is true of God is true of man. God can't possibly be blind, deaf, dumb, or sick. The Truth about man is that the Living Spirit Almighty is within him. God is all Bliss, Wholeness, Joy, Perfection, Harmony, and Peace. God is all the wonderful things you have ever heard of. There cannot possibly be any quarrel or division in this Boundless Wisdom. As you anchor your mind on these Eternal Verities about God, identify yourself with them mentally and a rearrangement of the thought-patterns

81

will take place in your mind and the Wholeness and Perfection of God will be made manifest.

The *clay* spoken of is a hard, dry, false belief. It is a muddy, confused mind which must be cleansed; then we *spit* (bring forth) our conviction of Truth.

Go wash in the pool of Siloam means give up and send away. Detach your consciousness from the old state which washes away the false idea and feel and affirm the spirituality of all substance. The blind state also represents our inability to see the state that would bless us. When man does not know that his savior is the realization of his heart's desire, he is truly blind.

We might also mention in this chapter dealing with the man born blind that all men are born blind. We are born into all that our environment represents. We have to learn how to choose and differentiate so that gradually we awaken to the Presence and Power of God within us.

There is a tendency among people to take everything literally. In your daily newspaper you may see a cartoon depicting some extravagance or waste in Government. You understand it as an allegorical picture of things, that is, visual allegory. We must remember that the Bible is an allegory in words. When people read of the blind, the halt, and the lame in the Bible they usually think of it only from the physical side.

We must see that there is also an internal deafness and an inner blindness though the eyes and ears may not be impaired or diseased in any way. A man can be psychologically lame when he is afraid to take on a new project. In some instances men refuse promotion because they are afraid they might fail. This is lameness even though the physical legs are perfect.

Dr. Nicoll of England stresses the fact that the transformation of meaning from the sensual or sensory level to the emotional and mental level is an act of faith.

For we walk by faith, not by sight: 2 Cor. 5:7. Most people "walk by sight," that is, the literal meaning of everything dominates their consciousness. The blind man is the one who is blind inside.

In *Matthew* we read: *And, behold, two blind men sitting by the way side, when they heard that Jesus passed by, cried out, saying, Have mercy on us, O Lord, thou son of David. And the multitude rebuked them, because they should hold their peace: but they cried the more, saying, Have mercy on us, O Lord, thou son of David. And Jesus stood still, and called them, and said, What will ye that I shall do unto you? They say unto him, Lord, that our eyes may be opened. So Jesus had compassion on them, and touched their eyes: and immediately their eyes received sight, and they followed him.* Matt. 20:30-34.

The two blind men refers to the average man who walks the earth because he is intellectually and emotionally blind. We have a conscious and subconscious mind, i.e., two phases or functions of the One Mind in all. If we do not consciously choose good thoughts and meditate on the lovely and beautiful, our intellect is blind. If we fail to realize and draw forth the wisdom, intelligence, and power of the subjective self, we are blind to the Kingdom of Heaven within.

A *blind man* thinks that hard work will make him wealthy. He fusses, frets, and fumes because he doesn't know that wealth is simply a state of consciousness. The feeling of wealth produces wealth; the feeling of health produces health. Confidence in the One Eternal Source and aligning ourselves mentally with it will take the form of wealth, health, peace, and all the blessed things of life.

I just spoke with a young actress who receives a thousand dollars a week for a few hours work each week. She said there were other actresses far prettier, more attractive, better educated than she, getting a hundred or a hundred and fifty dollars a week in small parts. Her explanation was that they had a low estimate of themselves and lacked confidence. They were blind and did not know that if we make a bargain with life for a penny a day, that is what we will receive. If they would overcome their estimate of themselves and claim their good in consciousness, there would be an automatic response, for *according to your belief is it done unto you.*

A few hours ago I chatted with a man who is leaving this city to take a sales manager job in San Francisco. Last month he was getting meager wages according to some union scale. *His eyes were opened* in our recent class on the inner meaning of the book of *Job*. He began to picture himself receiving congratulations from his wife on his marvelous promotion. He kept running the picture in his mind until it was fully developed in the subconscious, and much to his delight the promotion was confirmed objectively. The two blind states in him began to see because he brought about a harmonious union of his conscious and subconscious mind. These two phases synchronized and agreed on promotion, and what he subjectively felt as true became an objective manifestation. The cry of the world is *Lord, that out eyes may be opened. Jesus* is your awareness of the Spiritual Power within you and your capacity to use it so that you can rise above any predicament or limitation.

The Bible says, *Jesus touched their eyes.* When you touch something you become aware of it as a sensation, a feeling. You have made contact, so to speak. You touch the Spiritual Power or the Presence of God with your thought, your mental picture.

And immediately their eyes received sight. This means that you will get an immediate response from the Spirit within you whose nature is responsiveness. You now receive your sight because you mentally perceive and lay hold of the Spiritual Power within you. You comprehend its nature and give it your sole allegiance and loyalty. The Maker of your eyes can heal your eyes.

Jesus is always *passing by* for the simple reason that your desire is your Jesus. Every problem has its solution or savior in the form of a desire. The desire is walking down the streets of your mind now. There is a *multitude* of fears, doubts, and anxious thoughts which challenges your desire and divides your allegiance. This is the *multitude* which, according to the parable, tries to restrain the blind men. *But they cried the more*, meaning that you must dynamically and decisively break through that motley crew of negative thoughts in your mind. You must push them all aside and have eyes only for your savior, i.e., your desire.

Set your desire on high; love it; be loyal to it; kiss it affectionately; let it captivate you. You are now being loyal and you will succeed in touching the Healing Presence. At the moment you touch it, the Infinite Healing Power flows through the channel you created and your prayer is answered.

We should not ask for more Light. Rather, our prayer should be, "O God, give me eyes to see the Light." The Light of God always was, now is, and ever shall be. It is wonderful.

Chapter

10

WALK WITH THE POWER OF GOD

*After this there was a feast of the Jews; and Jesus went up to Jerusalem.
Now there is at Jerusalem by the sheep market a pool, which is called in the
Hebrew tongue Bethesda, having five porches. In these lay a great multitude
of impotent folk, of blind, halt, withered, waiting for the moving of the water.
For an angel went down at a certain season into the pool, and troubled the
water: whosoever then first after the troubling of the water stepped in was made
whole of whatsoever disease he had. And a certain man was there, which had
an infirmity thirty and eight years. When Jesus saw him lie, and knew that he
had been now a long time in that case, he saith unto him, Wilt thou be made
whole? The impotent man answered him, Sir, I have no man, when the water
is troubled, to put me into the pool: but while I am coming, another steppeth
down before me. Jesus saith unto him, Rise, take up thy bed, and walk.* John
5:1-8. *Related passages,* Luke 13:11-12.

Mankind is at the *pool.* The *pool* is consciousness, and all of
us are living with our thoughts, feelings, beliefs, opinions, and
mental images. Some of these states are *blind, halt, withered,* and
lame. Furthermore, man is full of dreams, hopes, and aspirations
which have never seen the light of day. Thousands are frustrated,
unhappy, and sick because they have failed to realize their dreams,
ideals, plans, and purposes. These dead hopes and dreams
symbolize the *impotent folk, blind, halt, withered, waiting for the moving
of the water.*

Are you waiting for something to happen? Don't sit around waiting for God to do something. You must begin, and when you begin Omnipotence begins to move on your behalf. God has provided you with everything. He has given you Himself; therefore, all His powers, qualities, and attributes are within you, waiting for you to call them forth and use them to grow.

Expand, unfold, and multiply your good a thousandfold. The initiative is with you. The God-Presence within is now governing all your vital organs, regulating your heart beat and general circulation. The earth, the stars, the sun, and moon, and the whole world is here for you to enjoy, but if you want to transcend your present concept of yourself, you must take the necessary steps.

Begin now to think constructively and heal the *blind, deaf,* and *withered* states within you. In this drama of healing, prayer is called a *feast.* When you meditate on your good, you are *feasting,* i.e., you are consciously uniting with it; then you make it a living part of you in the same manner that a piece of bread becomes hair on your face or flesh of your body.

The pool has five porches which means we have five senses. Our senses usually deny what we pray for; furthermore, our five senses impregnate us with all kinds of rumors, false beliefs, and limitations.

Now you can put into application the teaching of this drama. You are *Jesus* when you recognize the Spiritual Power within as Omnipotent, and you enter *Jerusalem* (city of peace) when you still the mind and focus on the Living Spirit Almighty within you. You are now back at your Divine Center where you become perfectly quiet in God. You can enter into a deep peace, the Peace of God. You have exchanged the mood of worry and fear for the mood of faith, confidence, and an inner peace. This is why the Bible refers to a *sheep market.* All of us are in the market place every moment of our lives. You are constantly exchanging or giving up one idea for another. You must give up fear and buy faith in God and His Laws. Give up ill will and buy radiant good will. Give up the *blind states* in your belief and buy the idea that there is a way out of any problem. Contemplate the Truth that God has the answer, and therefore you know the answer.

The angel disturbs the pool. The *angel* spoken of is your desire, your wish. A man in our class on the "Miracles of Healing," on which this book is based, told me of a wrong done to him. He was very bitter. He had a desire for a Divine adjustment, but didn't know how to bring it about, and he was very disturbed. He learned how to resolve the conflict. *Whosoever stepped in first was made whole.* No one could get in before him. He was always in the Holy Omnipresence and he perceived the Truth that actually no one could really rob him or defraud him. When he learned of his Oneness with God and the fact that nothing can be lost, he realized his unity with the Infinite. He prayed that through the action of God his relationship with the other man was now transformed into order, harmony, goodness, and love. He began to see as God sees, and God sees everything in Infinite Perfection.

In other words, this young man ceased to gaze at the outward chaos and confusion, but he went within himself and claimed interior harmony and a Divine adjustment. The blurred, confused, outer picture was transformed into Divine order and peace between them. There was a remarkable solution. Trust the God-Wisdom which knows all and knows the way. "There's a Divinity that shapes our ends, Rough-hew them how we will."

In one of the class-lessons on the book of *Job,* which I have just finished, I told the students that if they had a problem, and could not see any way out, to sit still that night and quietly recognize the Presence of God within themselves, in the situation itself, and within all those concerned. After a few minutes of silent contemplation on that Truth, they were to turn the matter over completely to the subjective self, knowing it will order everything aright. This procedure kindles a fire in the heart which brings about an inner glow and warmth; and while this fire of love is burning in the heart, go off to sleep. Many received remarkable answers the next morning.

No one really can *get in before you.* No one can prevent you from realizing your goal or objective. The only power you are aware of is your own thought. When you think, that process is really Omnipotence in action. One with God is a majority. Your own thought causes the Omnipotent Power of God to move in your behalf. There is nothing to oppose, challenge, or thwart the action of the Infinite One. There can't be two omnipotent powers; if there were, one would cancel and neutralize the action of the other and there would be no order anywhere. There can't be two Infinites, that is unthinkable and mathematically impossible.

The Infinite moves, Troward tells you, as unity, as oneness, as wholeness, and as harmony. Your mind must also move as a unity, a sense of oneness with your ideal. If you are divided in your mind by acknowledging some other power, you are like a soldier marking time, you get nowhere and reach an impasse. Your mind is divided, two ideas or thoughts are quarreling. You must be the referee and come to a decision by realizing that there is but One Power; and that being so, you are free from fear. Desire without fear is realization.

Recall to mind that the suggestions of others, the race mind and its fears have no power over you. External conditions and suggestions of others are not causative. Your thought is in control. If you say that the other hurt you or made you angry, it means you permitted yourself to move in thought negatively. It was your fault and not the other person's. The other person is certainly not responsible for the way you think about him or the way you think in general. When you think of God, you are one with Omnipotence. The Source is Love; It knows no fear.

While I am coming, another steppeth down before me. Have you ever said that? Perhaps not, but you have heard people say, "It was John's fault," "Except for Mary or Johnny I would have been promoted." If you say anything of that nature, your allegiance is divided and you are disloyal to the One Power which knows no other. *I am God and there is no God beside me.*

I am sure that you are very familiar with the fact that no one can say *I AM* for you. That statement is in the first person, present tense. It means you are announcing the Presence of God within as Cause and Creator. Notice when you speak to your sister or son you say, "You are."

When you speak in the third person you say, "They are."

One of our students in the Bible class on the book of *John* said to herself, "I possess the power to say 'I AM.' No one can say it for me. I now believe I AM what I wish to be. I live, move, and have my being in that mental atmosphere and no person, place, or thing can get in before me or prevent me from being what I long to be; for, *according to my belief, is it done unto me*." She had a remarkable demonstration using the above prayer.

The *impotent man is* the man who does not know where the power is and believes it is outside himself. The *thirty and eight years* in the numerical symbology or science of the Bible means the conviction of God's Presence and coming of age spiritually. The number *thirty* refers to the Trinity or the creative working of our own mind; the *eight* means the octave or man's capacity to rise higher through knowledge of mental and spiritual laws. The Trinity is your thought and feeling and from the fusion of these comes the third step which is the conviction of your good, or God. When your idea is mothered by feeling or emotion and the two become one, you are at peace, and God is Peace. You are constantly putting the Trinity into operation. Ouspensky used to call the third element which entered in the neutral element. We call it God.

The idea of perfect health can be resurrected by you as you now claim, feel, and believe that the Healing Principle is instantly transforming your whole being into God's Perfect Pattern of harmony, health, and peace.

I read a remarkable article which appeared in the magazine *Nautilus* some years ago. It was written by Frederick Elias Andrews of Indianapolis. He said that as a boy he was pronounced incurable. He began to pray and from a crooked, twisted, cripple going about on hands and knees, he became a strong, straight, well-formed man. This young man decided what he wanted and that was a perfect healing. He created his own affirmation, mentally absorbing the qualities he needed. He affirmed over and over again: "I am whole, perfect, strong, powerful, loving, harmonious, and happy." He persevered and said that this prayer was the last thing on his lips at night and the first thing in the morning. He prayed for others also by sending out thoughts of love and health. This attitude of mind and way of prayer returned to him multiplied. Like Job of old who prayed for his friends, God gave him twice as much as he had before. His faith and perseverance paid off big dividends. Negative thoughts came to him but he did not entertain them. When thoughts of anger, jealousy, fear, or worry came into his mind, he would start his affirmation going in his mind. The answer to all fearful thoughts is to turn on the lamp of love forever burning in your heart.

The man in the Bible had the infirmity *thirty and eight years*. We have already discussed the Trinity. The number *eight* is added when healing takes place. *Eight* is composed of two circles representing the synchronous or harmonious interaction of your conscious and subconscious mind, or idea and feeling. When your desire and your emotional nature agree, there is no longer any quarrel between the two, and a healing follows.

The command by Jesus, or your own illumined reason, *Rise, take up thy bed and walk*, is your voice of authority, based on your inner conviction telling you that you are healed. We can actually hear the inner sound of our belief. It is veritably a command on the inside. You have *taken up your bed* (truth) and walk the earth a free man. All this happens on the *sabbath*.

The *sabbath* is an inner certitude or inner stillness which follows true prayer. It is really a state of mind in which you are unconcerned, unmoved, and undisturbed, because you know that just as surely as the sun rises in the morning there will be a resurrection of your desire. When you have reached the point of complete mental acceptance, you *are resting in the sabbath* or in the conviction "It is done." *And it was on the sabbath day he was healed.*

Chapter

11

THE IMPOSSIBLE MADE POSSIBLE

I shall give the highlights of the wonderful healing technique in the raising of Lazarus mentioned in Chapter Eleven of *John.* For a complete, detailed interpretation of this wonderful chapter, I recommend my book *Peace Within Yourself,* which is an interpretation, chapter by chapter, of the book of *John.*

Lazarus represents any dead state, the desire, plan, enterprise, or goal which is frozen within and has not been made alive and resurrected in your world of experience. It may also represent your desire for health which has failed to materialize.

Jesus at the grave of Lazarus represents you and your awareness of the Power which can resurrect your ideal which has been covered with the *grave clothes* of fear, doubt, and anxiety for a long time, and has been *suppressed in the tomb* of the subconscious.

Jesus said, Take ye away the stone. The stone of superstition, fear, and ignorance must be removed. *Martha,* representing the worldly viewpoint says to you, "*By this time he stinketh: for he hath been dead four days.*" Four represents the completed state, the termination, the manifestation. According to sense-evidence the situation seems absolutely hopeless, or the condition may seem to be incurable. Regardless of the external circumstances, even though the whole world would deny what you pray for, *if thou wouldest believe, thou shouldest see the glory of God.*

In other words, if you will turn away from sense-evidence and go within and contemplate the reality of what you pray for, and sing the song of triumph, you will see the Glory of God—you will see the answer to your prayer. *To believe* is to live in the state of being or having what you pray for. Your thought is your belief, and whatever you think, you become. Live with the thought and reality of the answered prayer, and there will be an atomic and molecular change in the diseased body to conform to the new mental pattern.

The stone is lifted as you positively refuse to give power to sickness, disease, or fear. As you give all power to God, *the stone is removed* and you are no longer weighted down with the burdens of the world. Your new mental attitude is *the angel who rolls away tire stone* of fear and false belief.

You are now *Jesus, lifting up your eyes saying, Father, I thank thee that thou hast heard me. And I knew that thou hearest me always. He cried with a loud voice, Lazarus, come forth.* John 11:41-43. These latter verses give a magnificent formula for prayer. The thankful attitude works miracles.

Many years ago, a friend of mine who had tuberculosis took these wonderful words of the Bible, *I thank thee Father that thou hast heard me, and I knew that thou hearest me always.* He reasoned it out this way. His human father always gave him whatever he promised him. At one time his father promised him a trip to France (he lived in Ireland). The trip was to take place in August, but the promise was made in May. He remembered how joyous and enthusiastic he was. He recalled bubbling over with expectancy and being thrilled beyond words. This happened even though the trip had not taken place. All he had was the promise; he knew it was certain because his father never failed him.

He said to himself, "Why shouldn't I be thankful and grateful to my Heavenly Father for the promise of perfect health, for know that he heareth me always, 'I will restore health unto thee and I will heal thee of thy wounds saith the Lord.'" Two or three times a day he would still his mind, relax, and let go. Then he would imagine he was talking to the Invisible Healing Presence within, and he began to whisper, "Thank you," over and over again. He did this until his mind was saturated with the feeling of thankfulness. At the end of three weeks the sputum test and all the others were completely negative. He cast God's Spell over himself. He became magnetized as he contemplated the harmony and perfection of God which he knew would be experienced by him, as it was already given to him by God. When he contemplated the Peace, Order, and Healing Power of God within him, there was a complete rearrangement of the atoms of his body. He became like a magnetized piece of steel which draws to itself other steel, and not nickel and other metals. In the diseased state he was demagnetized, the atoms were still present, but he ceased to vibrate harmony, health, and peace. His feeling of thankfulness and sense of confidence in the One Healing Power drew like a magnet the conviction that made him healthy, vital, harmonious, and whole.

Like the man mentioned above, give up the false belief that other powers can make you ill without your consent. Contemplate yourself the way you want to be, happy, healthy, radiant, and strong. Identify yourself with these qualities, and accept nothing else. Give up completely all fear in any other so-called causes or powers. Reject categorically and dynamically all false beliefs. Turn in confidence to the Supreme Power within which moves as your feeling, your faith, and trust. When you do this, you are becoming a marvelous mental and spiritual magnet and you will inevitably attract harmony, health, peace, and joy.

The three steps in *raising Lazarus from the dead are:*

1. Recognition of your consciousness as supreme cause.
2. Accept the idea of perfect health and live with it in your mind. To believe is to live with the idea, i.e., make it alive.
3. The inevitable conviction which follows the previous two steps. You are now filled with the feeling of being what you want to be.

Your mood is now one of authority and you say inwardly, *Lazarus, come forth.*

This is the command from the inside of the one who knows that *I and my Father are one.*

Chapter

12

A PRAYER FOR HEALING

A personal healing will ever be the most convincing evidence of the power of prayer. About thirty-five years ago I resolved a malignancy by using a prayer based on the 139th Psalm. I had just heard an interpretation of the Psalm and was meditating intensely on its profundity.

For thou hast possessed my reins: thou hast covered me in my mother's womb. I will praise thee; for I am fearfully and wonderfully made: marvelous are thy works; and that my soul knoweth right well. My substance was not hid from thee, when I was made in secret, and curiously wrought in the lowest parts of the earth. Thine eyes did see my substance, yet being imperfect; and in thy book all my members were written, which in continuance were fashioned, when as yet there was none of them.

This magnificent, inspired Psalm teaches that the body and its organs are formed in idea before it is made manifest, just as surely as we can observe that a watchmaker has the idea first in mind before the watch becomes an objective reality. Creative Intelligence fashions and molds the entire body. The Intelligence that creates the body must know how to heal it; furthermore, the Psalm states that *in thy book all my members were written*. The *book* is the Life Principle where the archetype of all organs are inscribed.

Using this Psalm as a basis for my prayer, I prayed in a very simple way as follows:

"My body was made in secret by God. His Wisdom fashioned all my organs, tissues, muscles, and bones. His Healing Power saturates my mind and body, making me whole and perfect. I will give thanks unto thee. Wonderful are thy works."

I prayed aloud for about five minutes two or three times a day, repeating this simple prayer. In about three months my skin was whole and perfect.

Wonderful are thy works; and that my soul knoweth right well.

THE MIRACULOUS
LAW OF HEALING

MURPHY ON QUIMBY

PHINEAS PARKHURST QUIMBY once called on a woman who was aged, lame, bound down, and on crutches. He states that her ailment was due to the fact that she was imprisoned by a creed so small and contracted that she could not stand upright or move ahead. She was living in a tomb of fear and ignorance; furthermore, she was taking the Bible literally, and it frightened her. In this tomb, Quimby said, the presence of God was trying to burst the bars, break through the bands, and rise from the dead. When the woman would ask other people for an explanation of some passage of the Bible, the answer would be as a stone, and she would hunger for the bread of life. Dr. Quimby diagnosed her case as a mind cloudy and stagnated due to excitation and fear, caused by inability to see clearly the meaning of the scriptural passages she had been reading. This condition showed itself in her body by a heavy and sluggish feeling, which would terminate in paralysis.

Quimby asked the woman what was meant by, "Yet a little while I am with you, and then I go unto him that sent me." She replied that it meant that Jesus went to heaven. Quimby made plain what the passage really meant by interpreting that being with her "a little while" meant his explanation of her symptoms, feelings, and their cause—that is, he had compassion and sympathy for her momentarily, but he could not remain in that mental state; the next step was to go to "him that sent me," which is the presence of God in all men.

Quimby immediately traveled in his mind and contemplated

perfect health, which is a part of God. He said to the woman, "Therefore, where I go, you cannot come, for you are in Calvin's belief, and I am in health." This explanation produced an instantaneous sensation in the woman, and a change came over her mind. She walked without her crutches. She had been, as it were, dead in error, and to bring her to life or truth was to raise her from the dead. "I quoted the resurrection of Christ and applied it to her own Christ or health; it produced a powerful effect on her." (The Quimby Manuscripts.)

Apply this principle of healing in your own life. Suppose, for instance, that your son were sick. Go within to him who sent you. God, or Life, sent all of us into the world. God is all bliss, harmony, peace, beauty, wisdom, and perfection. Turn within in thought, and quietly realize that the wisdom and infinite intelligence of God are right within you. The living intelligence and power of God sent you into this world, and fashioned all your organs from its own invisible pattern. You are now turning to the maker of your body. You are relaxed, at peace, poised, calm. You are full of confidence that the Creator of your body and mind can create and refashion your body according to his own divine pattern.

You have seen your son sick and in pain, but now in your meditation you are talking to the God-presence, calling forth the healing power. Think of your son, and immediately dwell on the peace, health, and harmony of God. You know that these qualities, potencies, and aspects of God are now being reflected in your boy. You are now getting into the mental atmosphere of health. As did Quimby, you are contemplating the Divine Ideal, which is perfection, wholeness, and harmony for your son. Do this frequently, three or four times daily, until you believe in the idea of perfect health. When you have mentally accepted the idea that the healing power of God is working for your son, that is a treatment.

"Ye shall seek me, and shall not find me," means that others may wonder what you are doing and be unable to follow you in understanding or belief. "And where I am, thither ye cannot come." Other members of your family, or the patient himself, may be unable to rise in consciousness and enter into the feeling of perfect health, because they are wrapped up in worldly beliefs. Quimby said that man's false belief is the sepulcher in which the wisdom of God is confined, and that the truth is the angel which rolls away the stone of superstition and ignorance, healing the mind and body.

The word "treatment" used in New Thought circles means the harmonious interaction and direction of the conscious and subconscious powers for a definite, specific purpose. In treating others or ourselves, we never identify with the disease. We have compassion for the person momentarily—"Yet a little while I am with you"; then we go to God and heaven, realizing the ideal perfection of the patient. The pharisaical beliefs (fear and doubt) cannot enter where confidence in God's power is. In prayer we are one with God, the only presence and power.

Here is an instance of how a woman applied this technique in the treatment of her child. Her child was very ill, and hope of saving his life had been given up by all except the mother. She sat by the child's hospital bed and prayed as follows: "God is the life of my child, and His healing power is flowing through every atom of his being. The peace of God floods his mind and body, and through His power my child is made whole." She silently repeated this simple prayer over and over again, trying to lift up the idea of health in her mind. She knew intuitively and instinctively as she continued praying that she would reach the point of inner peace about her boy. After a few hours, the child began to cry for food. The doctor examined the child and said he had passed the crisis. She had realized the truth which set her child free.

Our reason and senses may question, ridicule, scoff, and laugh, but if we will only go within, knowing that when we feel something as true, Omnipotence moves in our behalf—then, though the whole world would deny it, we would demonstrate our desire, because we are sealed in faith. "According to your faith be it unto you."

THE MIRACULOUS LAW OF HEALING

There is only one healing power. It is called by many names, such as God, Infinite Healing Presence, Nature, Divine Love, Divine Providence, the Miraculous Healing Power, Life, Life Principle, as well as many others. This knowledge goes back into the dim recesses of the past. An inscription has been found written over an ancient temple which reads: "The doctor dresses the wound, and God heals the patient."

The healing presence of God is within you. No psychologist, minister, doctor, surgeon, priest, or psychiatrist heals anyone. For example, the surgeon removes a tumor, thereby removing the block and making way for the healing power of God to restore you. The psychologist or psychiatrist endeavors to remove the mental block and encourages the patient to adopt a new mental attitude which tends to release the Healing Presence, flowing through the patient as harmony, health, and peace. The minister asks you to forgive yourself and others and to get in tune with the Infinite by letting the healing power of love, peace, and good will flow through your subconscious mind, thereby cleansing all the negative patterns that may be lodged there.

This infinite healing presence of Life, which Jesus called "Father," is the healing agent in all diseases, whether mental, emotional, or physical.

This miraculous healing power in your subconscious mind, if scientifically directed, can heal your mind, body, and affairs of all disease and impediments. This healing power will respond to you regardless of your race, creed, or color. It does not care whether you belong to any church or whether you have any creedal affiliations or not. You have had hundreds of healings since you were a child. You can recall how this healing presence brought curative results to cuts, burns, bruises, contusions, sprains, etc., and, in all probability, like the author, you did not aid the healing in any way by the application of external remedies.

HEALED OF SPIRIT-VOICES

A few years ago a young man from a local university came to see me with the complaint that he was constantly hearing spirit-voices, that they made him do nasty things, and that they would not let him alone; neither would they permit him to read the Bible or other spiritual books. He was convinced that he was talking to supernatural beings.

This young man was clairaudient, and, not knowing that all men possess this faculty to some degree, he began to think it was due to evil spirits. His superstitious beliefs caused him to ascribe it to departed spirits. Through constant worry, he became a monomaniac on the subject. His subconscious mind, dominated and controlled by an all-potent but false suggestion, gradually took over control and mastery of his objective faculties, and his reason abdicated its throne. He was what you would call mentally unbalanced, as are all men who allow their false beliefs to obtain the ascendancy.

I explained to this university student that his subconscious mind is of tremendous importance and significance and that it can be influenced negatively and positively, but he had to make sure that he influenced it only positively, constructively, and harmoniously. The subconscious mind possesses transcendent powers, but it is at the same time amenable to good and bad suggestions. The explanation which I gave him made a profound impression on him.

I gave him the following written prayer which he was to repeat for ten or fifteen minutes three or four times a day:

God's love, peace, harmony, and wisdom flood my mind and heart. I love the truth, I hear the truth, and I know the truth that God is Love, and His love surrounds me, enfolds me, and enwraps me. God's river of peace floods my mind, and I give thanks for my freedom.

He repeated this prayer slowly, quietly, reverently, and with deep feeling, particularly prior to sleep. By identifying himself with harmony and peace, he brought about a rearrangement of the thought-patterns and imagery of his mind, and a healing followed. He brought about a healing of his mind by repetition of these truths, coupled with faith and expectancy.

My own prayer for him night and morning was as follows: "John is thinking rightly. He is reflecting Divine wisdom and Divine intelligence in all his ways. His mind is the perfect mind of God, unchanging and eternal. He hears the voice of God, which is the inner voice of peace and love. God's river of peace governs his mind, and he is full of wisdom, poise, balance, and understanding. Whatever is vexing him is leaving him now, and I pronounce him free and at peace."

I meditated on these truths night and morning, getting the "feel" of peace and harmony; at the end of a week this young man was completely free and at peace.

She Wasn't Expected to Live

Some time ago, a woman told me that her child had a very high fever and was not expected to live. The doctor had prescribed small doses of aspirin and had administered an antibiotic preparation. The mother, who was involved in a contemplated divorce action, was terribly agitated and emotionally disturbed. This disturbed feeling was communicated subconsciously to the child, and naturally, the child got ill. Children are at the mercy of their parents and are controlled by the dominant mental atmosphere and emotional climate of those around them. They have not yet reached the age of reason when they can take control of their own thoughts, emotions, and reactions to life.

The mother, at my suggestion, decided to become more at ease and relax her tensions by reading the 23rd Psalm, praying for guidance and for the peace and harmony of her husband. She poured out love and goodwill to him and overcame her resentment and inner rage. The fever of the child was due to the suppressed rage and anger of the mother, which was subjectively felt by the child and expressed as a high fever due to the excitation of the child's mind.

Having quieted her own mind, the mother began to pray for her child in this manner: "Spirit, which is God, is the life of my child. Spirit has no temperature; it is never sick or feverish. The peace of God flows through my child's mind and body. The harmony, health, love, and perfection of God are made manifest in every atom of my child's body now. She is relaxed and at ease, poised, serene, and calm. I am now stirring up the gift of God within her, and all is well."

She repeated the above prayer every hour for several hours. Shortly thereafter, she noticed a remarkable change in her child, who awakened and asked for a doll and something to eat. The temperature became normal. What had happened? The fever left the little girl because the mother was no longer feverish or agitated in her mind. Her mood of peace, harmony, and love was instantaneously felt by the child, and a corresponding reaction was produced.

The Natural-Born Healer

We are all "natural-born healers" for the simple reason that the healing presence of God is within all men, and all of us can contact it with our thoughts. It responds to all. This Healing Presence is in the dog, the cat, the tree, and the bird. It is omnipresent and is the life of all things.

Degrees of Faith

There are different degrees of faith. There is the man who, through faith, heals his ulcers, and another who heals a deep-seated, so-called incurable malignancy. It is as easy for the healing presence of God to heal a tubercular lung as it is to heal a cut on your finger. There is no great or small in the God that made us all; there is no big or little, no hard or easy. Omnipotence is within all men. The prayers of the man who lays his hand on another in order to induce a healing simply appeal to the cooperation of the patient's unconscious, whether the latter knows it or not, or whether he ascribes it to Divine intercession or not, and a response takes place; for according to the patient's faith is it done unto him.

A Case of Palsy

An old friend of mine in New York City suffered from palsy and tremors some years ago. His legs would become locked so that inability to move was experienced. Panic would ensue, and my friend would be frozen to the spot, even in the middle of a busy street. He got some mild relief from sedatives and antispasmodics which were prescribed by his physician; however, this condition of constant fear, panic, and foreboding was wearing him down. The following procedure was adopted.

The first step was to get him to see that there was a miraculous healing power within him which had made his body and which also could heal it. I suggested to him that he read the 5th Chapter of Luke, verses 1824, and a related passage, Mark 2:3-5, where Jesus said to the man with the palsy: *"Man, thy sins are forgiven thee . . . I say unto thee, Arise, and take thy couch, and go into thine house."*

He read these verses avidly and was deeply moved by them. I explained to him that the couch or bed mentioned in the Bible means the bed in which a man lies in his own mind. The paralyzed man in the Bible undoubtedly was lying down amidst the thoughts of fear, doubt, condemnation, guilt, and superstition. These thoughts paralyze the mind and body.

We are told that Jesus healed the man of palsy by forgiving him his sins. To *sin* is to miss the mark, the goal of health, happiness, and peace. You forgive yourself by identifying mentally and emotionally with your ideal and continuing to do so until it gets within you as a conviction or subjective embodiment. You are sinning also when you think negatively or if you resent, hate, condemn, or engage in fear or worry. You are always sinning when you deviate or run away from your announced goal or aim in life, which should always be peace, harmony, wisdom, and perfect health—the life more abundant.

My friend admitted to me that he was full of hatred toward a brother who had double-crossed him years ago in a financial deal.

He also was full of guilt and self-condemnation and he realized that, like the paralytic in the Bible, he could not be healed until his sins had been cancelled by simply forgiving himself and his brother. He admitted to himself that his physical condition was quite a problem, but that he didn't have to have it.

He turned to the healing presence of God within him and affirmed boldly:

> "I fully and freely forgive myself for harboring negative and destructive thoughts, and I resolve to purify my mind from now on. I surrender and release my brother to God, and wherever he is, I sincerely wish for him health, happiness, and all the blessing of God. I am now aligned with the Infinite Healing Power, and I feel Divine love flowing through every atom of my being. I know that God's love is now permeating and saturating my whole body, making me whole and perfect. I sense the peace that passeth understanding. My body is a temple of the living God, and God is in His holy temple and I am free. As he meditated on these truths, he gradually became reconditioned to health and harmony. As he changed his mind, he changed his body. Changed attitudes change everything. Today he walks joyously and freely, completely healed."

He Healed His Withered Hand

An irate young man came to interview me, stating that his boss had fired him and had said to him, "You're like the man in the Bible with the withered hand." He said to me, "What did he mean? My hands are all right, they are perfectly normal." My explanation was as follows: In the correct interpretation of the Bible, it must be understood that principles are personified as persons in order to make portrayal and interaction vivid and forceful. We must not confine the story of the man with the withered hand to its literal meaning. The *hand* is a symbol of power, direction, and effectiveness. With your hand, you fashion, mold, direct, and design. Symbolically, a man has a withered hand when he has an inferiority complex and feels guilty and inadequate, or is a defeatist. Such a man does not function efficiently and is not expressing his God-given powers.

This young man admitted that his dreams, ambitions, ideals, plans, and purposes were withered and frozen in his mind because he did not know how to bring them to pass. Not knowing the laws of mind and how to pray correctly, he found that his wonderful ideas died aborning in his mind, resulting in frustration and neurosis. He was stagnating, literally dying on the vine. Furthermore, he was demoting and depreciating himself. His attitude toward life was all wrong; moreover, he admitted that his work was shoddy and desultory.

His hand (his ability to achieve and to accomplish) withered by saying to himself, "If I had Joe's brains or his wealth . . . his connections . . . I could advance and be somebody. But look at me, just a nobody. I was born on the wrong side of the tracks. I must be satisfied with my lot. I have a withered hand."

A remarkable change took place in this man, however, when he decided to *stretch forth his hand* by enlarging his concept and estimate of himself. He formed a picture in his mind of what he wished to achieve, i.e., to direct a large organization and to be successful. He began to affirm frequently, "I can do all things, through the God-power which strengthens, guides, controls, and directs me. I realize that I am going where my vision is. I now turn with faith and confidence to the Infinite Intelligence within me, knowing that I am directed by an inner wisdom. I know in my heart that the God-power flows through the patterns of thought and imagery in my mind, and I am under a Divine compulsion to succeed."

As he identified himself mentally and emotionally with these new concepts, he went forward from promotion to promotion and is now general manager of a large corporation, his current salary exceeding $75,000 annually.

How the Hopeless Case Was Healed

Jesus commanded the dead man, ". . . *And he said, Young man, I say into thee, Arise. And he that was dead sat up, and began to speak.*" (Luke 7:14-15)

When it says *the dead man sat up and began to speak*, it means that when your prayer is answered you speak in a new tongue of joyous health, and you exude an inner radiance. Your dead hopes and desires speak when you bear witness to your inner beliefs and assumptions.

As a corollary to this, I would like to tell about a young man I saw in Ireland a few years ago. He is a distant relative. He was in a comatose condition; his kidneys had not functioned for three days. His condition had been pronounced hopeless when I went to see him, accompanied by one of his brothers. I knew that he was a devout Catholic, and I said to him, "Jesus is right here, and you see him. He is putting his hand out and is this moment laying his hand upon you."

I repeated this several times, slowly, gently, and positively. He was unconscious when I spoke and was not consciously aware of either of us. He sat up in bed, however, opened his eyes, and said to both of us, "Jesus was here; I know I am healed I shall live."

What had happened? This man's subconscious mind had accepted my statement that Jesus was there, and his subconscious projected that thought-form, i.e. this man's concept of Jesus was portrayed based on what he saw in church statues, paintings, etc. He believed that Jesus was there in the flesh and that he had placed his hands upon him.

The readers of my book, *The Power of Your Subconscious Mind*, are well aware of the fact that you can tell a man who is in a trance that his grandfather is here now and that he will see him clearly. He will see what he believes to be his grandfather. His subconscious reveals the image of his grandfather based on his subconscious memory picture. You can give the same man a post-hypnotic suggestion by saying to him, "When you come out of this trance, you will greet your grandfather and talk to him," and he will do exactly that. This is called a subjective hallucination.

The faith which was kindled in the unconscious of my Catholic relative, based on his *firm belief* that Jesus came to heal him, was the healing factor. It is always done unto us according to our faith, mental conviction, or just blind belief. His subconscious mind was amenable to my suggestion; his deeper mind received and acted upon the idea I had implanted in his mind. In a sense, you could call such an incident *the resurrection of the dead*. It was the resurrection of his health and vitality. According to his belief was it done unto him.

Blind Faith and True Faith

True faith is based on the knowledge of the way your conscious and subconscious minds function and on the combined harmonious functioning of these two levels of mind scientifically directed. Blind faith is healing without any scientific understanding whatsoever of the forces involved. The voodoo doctor or witch doctor in the jungles of Africa heals by faith, and so do the bones of dogs (believed to be the bones of saints by the believer), or anything else which moves man's mind from fear to faith.

In all instances—regardless of the technique, *modus operandi* process, incantation, or invocation offered to saints and spirits— it is the subconscious mind that does the healing. Whatever you believe is operative instantly in your subconscious mind.

Be like the little eight-year-old boy in our Sunday school. Eye drops were not clearing up his eye infection, and he prayed as follows: "God, you made my eyes. I demand action, I want healing now. Hurry up. Thank you." He had a remarkable healing because of his simplicity, spontaneity, and childlike faith in God. ". . . *Go, and do thou likewise.*" (Luke 10:37)

How to Give a Spiritual Treatment

Spiritual treatment means that you turn to the Indwelling God and remind yourself of His peace, harmony, wholeness, beauty, boundless love, and limitless power. Know that God loves you and cares for you. As you pray this way the fear gradually will fade away. If you pray about a heart condition, do not think of the organ as diseased as this would not be spiritual thinking. Thoughts are things. Your spiritual thought takes the form of cells, tissues, nerves, and organs. To think of a damaged heart or high blood pressure tends to suggest more of what you already have. Cease dwelling on symptoms, organs or any part of the body. Turn your mind to God and His love. Feel and know that there is only one healing Presence and Power, and to its corollary: *There is no Power to challenge the action of God.*

Quietly and lovingly affirm that the uplifting, healing, strengthening power of the healing Presence is flowing through you making you every whit whole. Know and feel that the harmony, beauty, and life of God manifest themselves in you as strength, peace, vitality, wholeness, and right action. Get a clear realization of this, and the damaged heart or other disease organ will be cured in the light of God's love.

"*. . . Glorify God in your body . . .*" (I Corinthians 6:20)

VERY PROFITABLE POINTERS

1. The healing power of God is within you. Remove any mental block and let the healing power flow through you.
2. A monomaniac is a man who permits his mind to be dominated and controlled by an all-potent but false suggestion.
3. When a mother is agitated and seething with inner turmoil and rage, this negative emotion is communicated to the subconscious of her child and can cause fever. Let God's river of peace flood the mind and heart, and the child's fever will abate and harmony will be restored.
4. All of us are natural-born healers because the Infinite Healing Presence is within us, and we can contact it with our thoughts and beliefs.
5. The miraculous healing power which made your body knows how to heal it. It knows all the processes and functions of your body. Trust the healing power, and accept a healing now.
6. You can recondition yourself to health and harmony as you meditate frequently on harmony, vitality, wholeness, beauty, and perfection.
7. In the Bible, principles are personified as persons in order to make portrayal and interaction vivid and forceful. You can overcome a feeling of inferiority by joining up with God and by sensing that one with God is a majority.

8. There are no incurable diseases. There are incurable people who believe they can't be healed, and according to their belief is it done unto them.

9. Faith healing is healing without any scientific understanding of the forces involved. Spiritual mind healing is the combined and harmonious functioning of your conscious and subconscious mind, scientifically directed for a specific purpose. In all instances, it is the subconscious mind that heals regardless of the technique or process used.

HOW YOU CAN FACE THE WORD
"INCURABLE" IN YOUR OWN LIFE

Don't let the word "incurable" frighten you. Realize that you are dealing with the Creative Intelligence which made your body and that, although some men will say that a healing is impossible, be assured that this infinite Healing Presence is instantly available, and you can always draw on its power through the creative law of your own mind. Make use of this power now and perform miracles in your life. Remember that a miracle cannot prove that which is impossible; it is a confirmation of that which is possible, for "... *with God all things are possible.*" (Matthew 19:26) "... *I will restore health unto thee, and I will heal thee of thy wounds, saith the Lord* ..." (Jeremiah 30:17)

The word "Lord" in the Bible means the creative law of your mind. There is a deep-lying, healing principle which permeates the entire universe, that flows through your mental patterns, images, and choices, and objectifies them in form. You can bring into your life anything you wish through this infinite healing principle which operates through your own mind.

You may use this universal healing principle for any particular purpose. It is not confined to healing of the mind or body. It is the same principle which attracts to you the ideal husband or wife, prospers you in business, finds for you your true place in life, and reveals answers to your most difficult problems. Through the correct application of this principle, you can become a great salesman, musician, physician, or surgeon. You can use it to bring harmony where discord exists, peace to supplant pain, joy in place of sadness, and abundance in place of poverty.

Healing of Dropsy

I knew a man in London, England, who was not only very religious but was completely free from any ill will or resentment. However, he saw his father die of dropsy, and it made a very deep and lasting impression on him; he told me that all his life since that event he feared that the same thing would happen to him. He also told me that his father by way of treatment used to be tapped with an instrument, and that the doctor would draw out large amounts of water from his abdominal area. This lingering fear, which was never neutralized, was undoubtedly the cause of his dropsical condition. He did not know the simple psychological truth which Dr. Phineas Parkhurst Quimby of Maine had elucidated about one hundred years ago. Dr. Quimby said that *if you believe something, it will manifest, whether you are consciously thinking of it or not.* This man's fear grew into a conviction that he would become a victim of the same disorder that had troubled his father. This explanation, however, helped the man considerably. He began to realize that he had accepted a lie as truth.

I pointed out to him that his fear was a perversion of the truth, a fear which had no real power because there is no principle behind disease. There is a principle of health, none of disease; a principle of abundance, none of poverty; a principal of honesty, none of deceit; a principle of mathematics, none of error; and a principle of beauty, none of ugliness. Fortunately, his belief was in the only power which controlled him, and he knew that his mind could be used negatively or positively.

He came to a definite conclusion in his mind by reasoning that the Healing Presence which made him was still with him and that his disease was due to a disordered group of disease soaked thoughts; thus he rearranged his mind to conform to the Divine pattern of harmony, health, and wholeness.

Before going to sleep at night, he would affirm with feeling and with deep meaning behind each word: "The Healing Presence is now going to work, transforming, healing, restoring, and controlling all processes of my body according to its wisdom and Divine nature. My entire system is cleansed, purified, and quickened by the vitalizing energy of God. Divine circulation, assimilation, and elimination operate in my mind and body. The joy of the Lord is my abiding strength. I am made every whit whole, and I give thanks."

He repeated this prayer every night for about thirty days. At the end of that time, his mind had reached a conviction of health, and his physician dismissed him as whole and perfect.

Steps in Healing

The first step in healing is not to be afraid of the manifest condition from this very moment. The second step is to realize that the condition is only the product of past thinking, which will have no more power to continue its existence. The third step is mentally to exalt the miraculous healing power of God within you.

This procedure instantly will stop the production of all mental poisons in you or in the person for whom you are praying. Live in the embodiment of your desire, and your thought and feeling will soon be made manifest. Do not allow yourself to be swayed by human opinion and worldly fears, but live emotionally in the belief that it is God in action in your mind and body.

SPIRITUAL BLINDNESS

Millions of people are "blind," i.e., they are psychological and spiritually "blind" because they do not know that they become what they think all day long. Man is spiritually and mentally "blind" when he is hateful, resentful, or envious of others. He does not know that he is actually secreting mental poisons which tend to destroy him.

Thousands of people are constantly saying that there is no way to solve their problems, and their situation is hopeless. Such an attitude is the result of spiritual blindness. Man begins to see spiritually and mentally when he gets a new understanding of his mental powers, and develops a conscious awareness that the wisdom and intelligence in his subconscious can solve all his problems.

Everyone should become aware of the inter-relationship and interaction of the conscious and subconscious mind. Persons who were once blind to these truths, after careful introspection, will now begin to see the vision of health, wealth, happiness, and peace of mind that can be theirs through the correct application of the laws of mind.

Vision is Spiritual, Eternal, and Indestructible

We do not create vision, rather we manifest or release it. We see through the eye, not with it. The cornea of the eye is stimulated by light waves from objects in space; through the optic nerve, these stimuli are carried to the brain. When the inner light, or intelligence, meets the outer light in this manner, by a process of interpretation, we see.

Your eyes symbolize Divine love and a delight in the ways of God, plus a hunger and thirst for God's truth. Your *right eye* symbolizes right thought and right action. The left eye symbolizes God's love and wisdom. Think right and radiate good will to all, and you will focus perfectly.

. . . *Receive thy sight . . . And immediately he received his sight, and followed him, glorifying God . . .* (Luke 18:42-43)

Special Prayer for Eyes and Ears

I am the Lord that healeth me. My vision is spiritual, eternal, and a quality of my consciousness. My eyes are Divine ideas, and they are always functioning perfectly.

My perception of spiritual Truth is clear and powerful. The light of understanding dawns in me; I see more and more of God's Truth every day. I see spiritually; I see mentally; I see physically. I see images of Truth and Beauty everywhere.

The infinite Healing Presence is now, this moment, rebuilding my eyes. They are perfect, Divine instruments, enabling me to receive messages from the world within and the world without. The glory of God is revealed in my eyes.

I hear the Truth; I love the Truth; I know the Truth. My ears are God's perfect ideas, functioning perfectly at all times. My ears are the perfect instruments which reveal God's harmony to me. The love, beauty, and harmony of God flow through my eyes and ears; I am in tune with the Infinite. I hear the still, small voice of God within me. The Holy Spirit quickens my hearing, and my ears are open and free.

EIGHT HEALING STEPS

1. Man says it's impossible, but with God all things are possible. You can be healed by God, who created you.
2. The healing principle flows through your mental patterns of thought and imagery, bringing all things you wish into manifestation.
3. If you believe something, it will manifest—whether or not you are consciously thinking of it. Believe only in that which heals, blesses, and inspires you.
4. Exalt the power of God in the midst of you, and you will stop the spread of any disease in your body.
5. The thankful heart is close to God. Let all your prayers be made known with praise and thanksgiving.
6. You are spiritually blind when you don't know that thoughts are things, that what you feel you attract, and that what you imagine, you become.
7. Vision is spiritual, eternal, and indestructible. A wonderful prayer for the eyes is to affirm regularly: "I see better spiritually, mentally, and physically."
8. "*I will lift up mine eyes unto the hills, from whence cometh my help.*" (Psalm 121:1)

THE HEALING POWER OF LOVE

One of the most beautiful, soul-stirring stories in the Bible is the loving, moving account of Ruth and Boaz. **Ruth** means that which lovingly clings. **Boaz** means God's Truth. These are the two pillars which lead to the Holy of Holies within you.

You love God when you steadfastly refuse to give power to error and false beliefs, giving at the same time, all your allegiance and devotion to the Spiritual Principle within you, insisting that the Principle of Harmony be manifested in your life. When you mentally reject the power of the phenomenalistic world and give all your allegiance to the Spirit within as Omnipotent, knowing it is responsive to your thought, you have the Lord of Life as your shepherd and you are loving God because you are being loyal to the One Power.

Ruth said to her mother-in-law, Naomi, "Intreat me not to leave thee, or to return from following after thee: for whither thou goest, I will go: and where thou lodgest, I will lodge: thy people shall be my people, and thy God my God." Ruth 1:16

Naomi is the emotional self. The Bible says her two sons are dead, which means that the body and environment are expressing lack and limitation. When you are not manifesting or expressing the desires of your heart, you become frustrated and disappointed. This is a story about all of us. A woman's husband is dead, Biblically speaking, when the action of God has ceased to be expressed through her. She is no longer being impregnated by Divine Ideas such as Goodness, Truth, and Beauty. To put this in simple, psychological language, the emotions of defeat and despair are governing the consciousness. When a person lacks faith and confidence, and when initiative and the forward push are absent, truly the husband is dead. The woman in all of us is

131

our emotional or subjective nature. Thought is the husband, and feeling is the woman.

"Thy maker is thy husband." The male quality of the mind is your husband which means thought, action, desire, or the image-making faculty. When you are functioning spiritually, you desire to grow, expand, and move forward. Life is a progression. When the mind is sick and confused, the emotions are disturbed; in such a case the tendency is to withdraw within yourself and brood; then your ideas, dreams, and aspirations die within you, and you feel frustrated. Your present state of consciousness and your desire are your two sons. If you are healthy, happy, joyous, and prosperous, your two sons are alive. If you are full of fear and foreboding, and wallowing in the mire of despair and despondency, your two sons are dead. Naomi (mother-in-law, the emotional nature) may be full of despair; yet the spiritual urge within all of us pushes us to move on, to press on up higher. It is the Voice of God crying in the wilderness, saying to all men, "Make straight in the desert a highway for our God." Isaiah 40:2

Ruth represents that which lovingly clings to us. It is the Cosmic Urge, the Divine Impulse in all of us. It clings to us, haunts our minds, and is a persistent voice insisting upon our attention. Life is always seeking to express itself.

"Whither shall I go from thy spirit? Or whither shall I flee from thy presence?" Psalms 139:7. The Presence of God is in the sick man, in the man whose body is racked with pain. "Behold, I am there." There is something within man which reminds him of his origin and urges him back to it. It is his mission and purpose to cherish, enlarge, and liberate this memory so that it grows from a spark to a flame, and floods his whole being.

Ruth is called the female companion. She represents the unconscious desire of life to express itself and preserve itself at all costs. This inner female companion, or God in you, acts as a stimulus to your depressed state causing you to think and reason a way out of your dilemma. She could be called the mother in you, or the intuitive sense in you. All men want to be good, do good, and express good because their nature is divine. God is in all men seeking to express Himself through them. Every man is an incarnation of God, and when you have a desire to be greater than you are, it is God seeking to express that concept or urge through you. Relax, let go, adopt the mood of receptivity, and let God's fullness flow through you. "There is a Divinity which shapes our ends, rough hew them how we will."

Note carefully what Ruth in you says, "Whither thou goest, I will go; and where thou lodgest, I will lodge: thy people shall be my people, and thy God my God." For tender beauty, this statement is unsurpassed. Here is portrayed love, faith, and devotion to the end. "Where thou diest, I will die, and there will I be buried." Your faith in your ideal or goal must be maintained unto the end; then the old state dies and the new state (answered prayer) is resurrected. Ruth is really Life's urge seeking expression and progression through you. The journey is ever onward in consciousness. Ruth's urge in you is your love for God and all things spiritual. Fall in love with Wisdom, Truth, and Beauty, and wonders will take place in your life.

Boaz is the goal, the ideal you seek in life. You must have a goal in life, an aim, a purpose. You must be going somewhere, otherwise you simply drift aimlessly. Listen to Ruth, the inner promptings and murmurings of your heart strings. If you do not know what your true place in life is, pray for guidance, and you will get a lead such as a strong, persistent feeling or tendency in a certain direction. An idea may suddenly come to your mind like toast pops out of a toaster. The desire that lingers week in and week out is the true desire of your heart.

A boy of sixteen who recently prayed for guidance, for true expression in life, found himself joining religious groups, studying religious books, being interested in the Bible, etc. He plans to go to divinity school, and is very happy about it. Later on he will teach the laws of life and the way of the Spirit to all men. He prayed for guidance, so the deeper mind responded accordingly. If a certain premise is enthroned in the mind, the response must be the correlate of the premise. The premise and conclusion are one; the beginning and the end are the same; the seed and the plant are one. He had invoked the spirit of guidance, and having once invoked it and believed in it, he came under the spell of right action.

I talked to a man who was offered a position overseas. He could not accept because of his intense fear of water and airplanes. He became panic-stricken at the thought of getting on a boat. Undoubtedly there was a subconscious pattern behind this, a terrifying childhood experience, perhaps at the hands of some bully in the neighborhood pool. He had prayed for true expression, his prayer had been answered, but he said he could not accept.

There is away to overcome such fear. Ruth is the predominant part of the soul in man telling him there is always a way out, a solution. The mere fact that he came to see me regarding help for his problem showed that he knew instinctively there was away to overcome this fear. He was recognizing a Higher Power than his intellect.

He began to use his imagination constructively. He imagined and felt himself swimming in a pool, he felt the chill of the water, he made it vivid, real, and dramatic. He heard friends congratulate him on his progress. He became thoroughly immersed in the water mentally; it was a victorious, loving, interested movement of the mind.

He entered the water mentally until he was compelled to enter it physically. With the help of an instructor, he learned to swim and mastered the water. This was the working of the Spiritual Power Which he invoked. The Spiritual Power responded according to the nature of his invocation or prayer, and compelled him to respond; such is the law.

What we do on the inside, we experience on the outside. The Bible says, "Acquaint now thyself with Him, and be at peace, therefore good shall come to thee." Acquaint yourself with the mental and emotional operations of your own mind. Apply the principle of mind, realize your desire, and peace shall come unto thee.

Boaz means the Power and Wisdom of God. Boaz is that which blesses, heals, and makes you happy; Ruth (inner guidance) will lead you to it. It might be an invention you wish accepted, a desire to achieve in some field such as that of a singer, composer, great artist, or musician. Boaz is that which you wish to unite with in consciousness. You must marry Boaz. How do you marry or become one with your ideal (Boaz)? "Wash thyself therefore, and annoint thee, and put thy raiment upon thee." Ruth 3:3.

Your good is your God. *Wash thyself* means to cleanse your mind by refusing to give power to anything but your own consciousness, and the reigning power of your thought.

Refuse positively and definitely to let your mind dwell on any negative state. To lift up your ideal, is the meaning of *annoint thyself*. Look to your ideal, let the light shine on it, honor it, count it worthy, praise it, exalt it, tell yourself how wonderful your ideal is, and mentally accept it. Let your ideal captivate and enthrall you (wearing the garment). You will find a deific response within you. The Power or Principle within responds to your dominant thought and mood. It is called in modern science the law of action and reaction. You must fulfill certain conditions. There is something you must do before there is a divine response. Isaiah says, "Ask me of things to come concerning my sons, and concerning the works of my hand, command ye me."

God works through you; i.e., through your own thought and belief. In order for you to advance and grow spiritually, you must begin; then God begins. God will do nothing for you except through you. God works, of course, on a cosmic, universal scale in the control of call your vital functions and other body processes; beyond that you must initiate further growth and spiritual unfoldment. You must individualize and personalize the spirit in you.

The greatest study of man is man. This seems to be forgotten in our world today where we are feverishly engaged in building new hydrogen bombs. We must go back to God from whence we came. "So Boaz took Ruth, and she was his wife; and when he went in unto her, the Lord gave her conception, and she bare a son." Ruth 4:13. That son was to be the father of Jesse and the grandfather of David. When you come to God, to Truth, and to the Eternal Source, realizing the Source is Love, there is no fears only peace.

Begin now to meditate, to eat of the nourishing Truths of God which have stood the test of time. Feast on God's Love, Peace, Joy, Bliss, Beauty, and Perfection. Your mind will be nourished. Your soul will be fortified. God and His Peace will move on the waters of your mind. You will then be Ruth marrying Boaz, and you will give birth to a mental and spiritual child. He will be the father of the line of Jesse and David, meaning that you will experience the joy of the answered prayer—peace, health, and happiness.

Jesse means I AM or God, and *David* means Love. Your sense of union with God will be the progenitor or father of all things good in your world. Jesse (I AM), the awareness of the Presence of God, is born in your mind, and David, which is God's Love, rules your heart. You will have found your savior, your companion, your guide, your loving friend who will remain with you always. You will have arrived at the state of consciousness called Ruth when your human love is raised to Divine Love by detaching yourself from the false beliefs of the world, and by giving all your devotion and attention to the real spiritual values of life. In other words, you will be functioning as Ruth and Boaz by following always where Divine Love leads, and remaining steadfast in your belief and loyalty to the One Power.

Love in the highest and best degree, and acknowledge the God of Love as Lord of your life.

Such loyalty and devotion is always rewarded, and you will find yourself a ruler of your world full of joy, happiness, and peace. You will go from glory to glory, ever onward, upward, and Godward.

THE HEALING POWER OF YOUR
SUBCONSCIOUS MIND

Everyone is definitely concerned with the healing of bodily conditions and human affairs. What is it that heals? Where is this healing power? These are questions asked by everyone. The answer is that this healing power is in the subconscious mind of each person, and a changed mental attitude on the part of the sick person releases this healing power.

No mental or religious science practitioner, psychologist, psychiatrist, or medical doctor ever healed a patient. There is an old saying, "The doctor dresses the wound, but God heals it." The psychologist or psychiatrist proceeds to remove the mental blocks in the patient so that the healing principle may be released, restoring the patient to health. Likewise, the surgeon removes the physical block enabling the healing currents to function normally. No physician, surgeon, or mental science practitioner claims, "he healed the patient." The one healing power is called by many names—Nature, Life, God, Creative Intelligence, and Subconscious Power.

There are many different methods used to remove the mental, emotional, and physical blocks which inhibit the flow of the healing life principle animating all of us. The healing principle resident in your subconscious mind can and will, if properly directed by you or some other person, heal your mind and body of all disease. This healing principle is operative in all men regardless of creed, color, or race. You do not have to belong to some particular church in order to use and participate in this healing process. Your subconscious will heal the burn or cut on your hand even though you profess to be an atheist or agnostic.

The modern mental therapeutic procedure is based on the truth that the infinite intelligence and power of your subconscious mind responds according to your faith. Mental science practitioners or ministers follows the injunction of the Bible. They go into a private place, still their minds, relax, let go, and think of the infinite healing presence within them. They close their minds to all outside distractions as well as appearances, and then quietly and knowingly turns over a request or desire to the subconscious mind, realizing that the intelligence of the mind will provide answers according to specific needs.

The most wonderful thing to know is this: Imagine the end desired and feel its reality; then the infinite life principle will respond to your conscious choice and your conscious request. This is the meaning of *believe you have received, and you shall receive. This is* what the modern mental scientist does when practicing prayer therapy.

One process of healing

There is only one universal healing principle operating through everything—the cat, the dog, the tree, the grass, the wind, the earth—for everything is alive. This life principle operates through the animal, vegetable, and mineral kingdoms as instinct and the law of growth. The human mind is consciously aware of this life principle, and can consciously direct it to bless itself in countless ways.

There are many different approaches, techniques, and methods in using the universal power, but there is only one process of healing, which is faith, for *according to your faith is it done unto you.*

The law of belief

All religions of the world represent forms of belief, and these beliefs are explained in many ways. The law of life is belief. What do you believe about yourself, life, and the universe? *It is done unto you as you believe.*

140

Belief is a thought in your mind, which causes the power of your subconscious to be distributed into all phases of your life according to your thinking habits. You must realize the Bible is not talking about your belief in some ritual, ceremonial, form, institution, or formula. It is talking about belief itself. The belief of your mind is simply the thought of your mind. *If thou canst believe, all things are possible to him that believeth.* (Mark 9:23).

It is foolish to believe in something that will hurt or harm you. Remember, it is not the thing believed in that hurts or harms you, but the belief or thought in your mind that creates the result. All your experiences, all your actions, and all the events and circumstances of your life are but the reflections and reactions to your own thought.

Prayer therapy is the combined function of the conscious and subconscious mind scientifically directed

Prayer therapy is the synchronized, harmonious, and intelligent function of the conscious and subconscious levels of mind specifically directed for a definite purpose. In scientific prayer or prayer therapy, you must know what you are doing and why you are doing it. You trust the law of healing. Prayer therapy is sometimes referred to as mental treatment, or scientific prayer.

In prayer therapy you consciously choose a certain idea, mental picture, or plan which you desire to experience. You realize your capacity to convey this idea or mental image to your subconscious by feeling the reality of the state assumed. As you remain faithful in your mental attitude, your prayer will be answered. Prayer therapy is a definite mental action for a definite specific purpose.

Let's suppose that you decide to heal a certain difficulty by prayer therapy. You are aware that your problem or sickness, whatever it may be, must be caused by negative thoughts charged with fear and lodged in your subconscious mind, and that if you can succeed in cleansing your mind of these thoughts, you will get a healing.

You, therefore, turn to the healing power within your own subconscious mind and remind yourself of its infinite power and intelligence and its capacity to heal all conditions. As you dwell on these truths, your fear will begin to dissolve, and the recollection of these truths also corrects the erroneous beliefs.

You give thanks for the healing that you know will come, and then you keep your mind off the difficulty until you feel guided, after an interval, to pray again. While you are praying, it is essential that you refuse to give any power to any negative conditions or to admit for a second that the healing will not come. This attitude of mind brings about the harmonious union of the conscious and subconscious mind, which releases the healing power.

Faith healing, what it means, and how blind faith works

What is popularly termed faith healing is not the faith mentioned in the Bible, which means a knowledge of the interaction of the conscious and subconscious mind. Faith healers are people who heal without any real scientific understanding of the powers and forces involved. They may claim that they have a special gift of healing, and the sick person's blind belief in these powers may bring results.

Voodoo doctors in primitive societies may heal by incantations, or a person may be healed by touching the so-called bones of saints, or anything else, which cause the patients to honestly believe in the method or process.

Any method which causes one to move from fear and worry to faith and expectancy will heal. There are many persons, who my claim that because a personal theory produces results, it is, therefore, the correct one. This, as already explained in this chapter, cannot be true.

To illustrate how blind faith works: Let's look at the Swiss physician, Franz Anton Mesmer. In 1776 he claimed many cures when he stroked diseased bodies with artificial magnets. Later on he threw away his magnets and evolved the theory of animal magnetism. This he held to be a fluid which pervades the universe, but is most active in the human organism.

He claimed that this magnetic fluid, which was going forth from him to his patients healed them. People flocked to him, and many wonderful cures were affected.

Mesmer moved to Paris, and while there the Government appointed a commission composed of physicians and members of the Academy of Science, of which Benjamin Franklin was a member, to investigate his cures. The report admitted the leading facts claimed by Mesmer, but held that there was no evidence to prove the correctness of his magnetic fluid theory, and said the effects were due to the imagination of the patients.

Soon after this, Mesmer was driven into exile, and died in 1815. Shortly afterwards, Dr. Braid of Manchester undertook to show that magnetic fluid had nothing to do with the production of the healings of Dr. Mesmer. Dr. Braid discovered that patients could be thrown into hypnotic sleep by suggestion, during which many of the well-known phenomena ascribed to magnetism by Mesmer could be produced.

You can readily see that all these cures were undoubtedly brought about by the active imagination of the patients together with a powerful suggestion of health to their subconscious minds. All this could be termed blind faith as there was no understanding in those days as to how the cures were brought about.

Subjective faith and what it means

You will recall the proposition, which need not be repeated at length, that the subjective or subconscious mind of an individual is as amenable to the control of his own conscious or objective mind as it is by the suggestions of another. It follows that whatever may be your objective belief, if you will assume to have faith actively or passively, your subconscious mind will be controlled by the suggestion, and your desire will be fulfilled. The faith required in mental healings is purely subjective.

In the healing of the body it is, of course, desirable to secure the concurrent faith of both the conscious and subconscious mind. However, it is not always essential if you will enter into a state of passivity and receptivity by relaxing the mind and the body and getting into a sleepy state. In this drowsy state your passivity becomes receptive to subjective impression.

Recently, I was asked, "How is it that I got a healing through a minister? I did not believe what he said when he told me that there is no such thing as disease and that matter does not exist."

This man at first thought his intelligence was being insulted, and he protested against such a palpable absurdity. The explanation is simple. He was quieted by soothing words and told to get into a perfectly passive condition, to say nothing, and think of nothing for the time being. His minister also became passive, and affirmed quietly, peacefully, and constantly for about one half hour that this man would have perfect health, peace, harmony, and wholeness. He felt immense relief and was restored to health.

It is easy to see that his subjective faith had been made manifest by his passivity under treatment, and the suggestions of perfect healthfulness by the minister were conveyed to his subconscious mind. The two subjective minds were then *en rapport*. The minister was not handicapped by antagonistic auto-suggestions of the patient arising from objective doubt of the power of the healer or the correctness of the theory. In this sleepy, drowsy state the conscious mind resistance is reduced to a minimum, and results followed. The subconscious mind of the patient being necessarily controlled by such suggestion exercised its functions in accordance therewith, and a healing followed.

The meaning of absent treatment

Suppose you learned that your mother was sick in New York City and you lived in Los Angeles. Your mother would not be physically present where you are, but you could pray for her. *It is the Father within which doeth the work.* (JOHN 14:10)

The creative law of mind (subconscious mind) serves you and will do the work. Its response to you is automatic. Your treatment is for the purpose of inducing an inner realization of health and harmony in your mentality. This inner realization, acting through the subconscious mind, operates through your mother's subconscious mind as there is but one creative mind. Your thoughts of health, vitality, and perfection operate through the one universal subjective mind, and set a law in motion on the subjective side of life that manifests through her body as a healing.

In the mind principle there is no time or space. It is the same mind that operates through your mother no matter where she may be. In reality there is no absent treatment as opposed to present treatment for the universal mind is omnipresent. You do not try to send out thoughts or hold a thought. Your treatment is a conscious movement of thought, and as you become conscious of the qualities of health, well-being, and relaxation, these qualities will be resurrected in the experience of your mother, and results will follow.

The following is a perfect example of what is called absent treatment. Recently, a listener of our radio program in Los Angeles prayed as follows for her mother in New York who had a coronary thrombosis: "The healing presence is right where my mother is. Her bodily condition is but a reflection of her thought-life like shadows cast on the screen. I know that in order to change the images on the screen I must change the projection reel. My mind is the projection reel, and I now project in my own mind the image of wholeness, harmony, and perfect health for my mother. The infinite healing presence which created my mother's body and all

145

her organs is now saturating every atom of her being, and a river of peace flows through every cell of her body. The doctors are divinely guided and directed, and whoever touches my mother is guided to do the right thing. I know that disease has no ultimate reality; if it had, no one could be healed. I now align myself with the infinite principle of love and life, and I know and decree that harmony, health, and peace are now being expressed in my mother's body."

She prayed in the above manner several times daily, and her mother had a most remarkable recovery after a few days, much to the amazement of her specialist. He complimented her on her great faith in the power of God.

The conclusion arrived at in the daughter's mind set the creative law of mind in motion on the subjective side of life, which manifested itself through her mother's body as perfect health and harmony. What the daughter felt as true about her mother was simultaneously resurrected in the experience of her mother.

Releasing the kinetic action of the subconscious mind

A psychologist friend of mine told me that one of his lungs was infected. X rays and analysis showed the presence of tuberculosis. At night before going to sleep he would quietly affirm, "Every cell, nerve, tissue, and muscle of my lungs are now being made whole, pure, and perfect. My whole body is being restored to health and harmony."

These are not his exact words, but they represent the essence of what he affirmed. A complete healing followed in about a month's time. Subsequent X rays showed a perfect healing.

I wanted to know his method, so I asked him why he repeated the words prior to sleep. Here is his reply, "The kinetic action of the subconscious mind continues throughout your sleep-time period. Hence, give the subconscious mind something good to work on as you drop off into slumber." This was a very wise answer. In thinking of harmony and perfect health, he never mentioned his trouble by name.

I strongly suggest that you cease talking about your ailments or giving them a name. The only sap from which they draw life is your attention and fear of them. Like the above mentioned psychologist, become a mental surgeon. Then your troubles will be cut off like dead branches are pruned from a tree. If you are constantly naming your aches and symptoms, you inhibit the kinetic action, which means the release of the healing power and energy of your subconscious mind. Furthermore, by the law of your own mind, these imaginings tend to take shape, *As the thing I greatly feared*. Fill your mind with the great truths of life and walk forward in the light of love.

Summary of your aids to health

1. Find out what it is that heals you. Realize that correct directions given to your subconscious mind will heal your mind and body.
2. Develop a definite plan for turning over your requests or desires to your subconscious mind.
3. Imagine the end desired and feel its reality. Follow it through, and you will get definite results.
4. Decide what belief is. Know that belief is a thought in your mind, and what you think you create.
5. It is foolish to believe in sickness and something to hurt or to harm you. Believe in perfect health, prosperity, peace, wealth, and divine guidance.
6. Great and noble thoughts upon which you habitually dwell become great acts.
7. Apply the power of prayer therapy in your life. Choose a certain plan, idea, or mental picture. Mentally and emotionally unite with that idea, and as you remain faithful to your mental attitude, your prayer will be answered.

8. Always remember, if you really want the power to heal, you can have it through faith, which means a knowledge of the working of your conscious and subconscious mind. Faith comes with understanding.

9. Blind faith means that a person may get results in healing without any scientific understanding of the powers and forces involved.

10. Learn to pray for your loved ones who may be ill. Quiet your mind, and your thoughts of health, vitality, and perfection operating through the one universal subjective mind will be felt and resurrected in the mind of your loved one.

MEDITATIONS & AFFIRMATIONS

For Health, Wealth, Relationships, and Self-Expression

INTRODUCTION

These pages are full of powerful affirmations for Health, Wealth, Relationships, and Self-Expression. The idea behind these techniques is pretty simple. Most of us grow up learning to put ourselves down for any real or imagined error. We grow up believing certain things about ourselves or comparing ourselves negatively to others. The use of positive affirmations is a technique to change negative self-talk into something more positive. Since we've spent many years on the negative image it's unreasonable to expect an instant effect from affirmations, but if we stick to it for a few days, with honesty, trust, and belief, results will start to happen.

CONSCIOUSNESS OF HEALTH

How to Apply the Healing Principle

I WILL RESTORE health unto thee, and I will heal thee of thy wounds, say the Lord. The God in me has limitless possibilities. I know that all things are possible with God. I believe this and accept it wholeheartedly now. I know that the God-Power in me makes darkness light and crooked things straight. I am now lifted up in consciousness by contemplating that God indwells me.

I speak the word now for the healing of mind, body, and affairs; I know that this Principle within me responds to my faith and trust. "The Father does the works." I am now in touch with life, love, truth, and beauty within me. I now align myself with the Infinite Principle of Love and Life within me. I know that harmony, health, and peace are now being expressed in my body.

As I live, move, and act in the assumption of my perfect health, it becomes actual. I now imagine and feel the reality of my perfect body. I am filled with a sense of peace and well-being. Thank you, Father.

The Healing Principle

Jesus said, "Thy faith hath made thee whole." I positively believe in the Healing Power of God within me. My conscious and subconscious minds are in perfect agreement. I accept the statement of truth which I positively affirm. The words I speak are words of spirit and they are truth.

I now decree that the healing Power of God is transforming my whole body making me whole, pure, and perfect. I believe with a deep, inner certitude that my prayer of faith is being manifest now. I am guided by the wisdom of God in all matters. The Love of God flows in transcendent beauty and loveliness into my mind and body, transforming, normalizing, and energizing every atom of my being. I sense the peace that passes through understanding. God's Glory surrounds me, and I rest forever in the Everlasting Arms.

Wearing His Garment

I have found God in the sanctuary of my own soul. God is Life; that Life is my life. I know God is not a body; He is shapeless, timeless, and ageless; I see God in my mind's eye. Through understanding I see and look upon God in the same way that I see the answer to a mathematical problem.

I now rise to the awareness of peace, poise, and power. This feeling of joy, peace, and goodwill within me is actually the spirit of God moving within me; It is God in action; It is Almighty.

There is no power in external things to hurt me; the only Power resides in my own mind and consciousness.

My body is the garment of God. The Living Spirit Almighty is within me; It is absolutely pure, holy, and perfect. I know that this Holy Spirit is God, and that this Spirit is now flowing through me healing and making my body whole, pure, and perfect. I have complete power over my body and my world.

My thoughts of peace, power, and health have the Power of God to be realized within me now. "Blessed are the pure in heart: for they shall see God." I have seen and felt His Holy Presence; it is wonderful.

The Quiet Mind

God dwells at the center of my being. God is Peace; this Peace enfolds me in its arms now. There is a deep feeling of security, vitality, and strength underlying this peace. This inner sense of peace, in which I now dwell, is the silent, brooding Presence of God. The Love and the Light of God watch over me, as a loving mother watches over the sleeping child. Deep in my heart is the Holy Presence that is my peace, my strength, and my source of supply.

All fear has vanished. I see God in all people; I see God manifest in all things. I am an instrument of the Divine Presence. I now release this inner peace; it flows through my entire being releasing and dissolving all problems; this is the peace that passes through understanding.

Mental Poise

"Whither shall I go from thy Spirit? Or whither shall I flee from thy Presence? If I ascend up into heaven, thou art there: if I make my bed in hell, behold, thou art there. If I take the wings of the morning, and dwell in the uttermost parts of the sea: Even there shall thy hand lead me, and thy right hand shall hold me." I am now full of a Divine enthusiasm, because I am in the Presence of Divinity. I am in the Presence of All Power, Wisdom, Majesty, and Love.

The Light of God illumines my intellect; my mind is full of poise, balance, and equilibrium. There is a perfect mental adjustment to all things. I am at peace with my own thoughts. I rejoice in my work; it gives me joy and happiness. I draw continually upon my Divine Storehouse; for it is the only Presence and the only Power. My mind is God's mind; I am at peace.

The Peace of God

All is peace and harmony in my world, for God in me is "The Lord of Peace." I am the consciousness of God in action; I am always at peace. My mind is poised, serene, and calm. In this atmosphere of peace and goodwill which surrounds me, I feel a deep abiding strength and freedom from all fear. I now sense and feel the love and beauty of His Holy Presence. Day by day I am more aware of God's Love; all that is false falls away. I see God personified in all people. I know that as I allow this inner peace to flow through my being, all problems are solved. I dwell in God; therefore, I rest in the eternal arms of peace. "Your life is hid with Christ in God." My peace is the deep, unchanging peace of God; "It is the peace of God, which passes through all understanding."

Spiritual Medicine

"A merry heart makes a cheerful countenance." The spirit of the Almighty pervades every atom of my being making me whole, joyous, and perfect. I know that all of the functions of my body respond to this inner joy welling up within me. I am now stirring up the gift of God within me; I feel wonderful. The oil of joy and illumination anoint my intellect, and become a lamp unto my feet.

I am now perfectly adjusted emotionally; there is a Divine equilibrium functioning in my mind, body, and affairs. I resolve from this moment forward to express peace and happiness to every person I meet. I know that my happiness and peace come from God; as I shed His light, love, and truth to others, I am also blessing and healing myself in countless ways. I radiate the sunshine of God's Love to all mankind. His Light shines through me and illuminates my path. I am resolved to express peace, joy, and happiness.

Controlling My Emotions

When a negative thought of fear, jealousy, or resentment enters my mind, I supplant it with the thought of God. My thoughts are God's thoughts, and God's Power is with my thoughts of good. I know I have complete dominion over my thoughts and emotions. I am a channel of the Divine. I now redirect all of my feelings and emotions along harmonious, constructive lines. "The sons of God shouted for joy." I now rejoice to accept the ideas of God which are peace, harmony, and goodwill, and I delight to express them; this heals all discord within me. Only God's ideas enter my mind, bringing me harmony, health, and peace. God is Love. Perfect Love casts out fear, resentment, and all negative states. I now fall in love with truth. I wish for all men everything I wish for myself; I radiate love, peace, and good will to all. I am at peace.

Overcoming Fear

There is no fear, as "perfect Love casts out fear." Today I permit Love to keep me in perfect harmony and peace with all levels of my world. My thoughts are loving, kind, and harmonious. I sense my oneness with God, for "In Him I live, move, and have my being."

I know that all of my desires will be realized in perfect order. I trust the Divine Law within me to bring my ideals to pass. "The Father does the works." I am divine, spiritual, joyous, and absolutely fearless. I am now surrounded by the perfect peace of God; it is "The peace of God which passes through all understanding." I now place all of my attention on the thing desired. I love this desire, and I give it my wholehearted attention.

My spirit is lifted into the mood of confidence and peace; this is the spirit of God moving in me. It gives me a sense of peace, security, and rest. Truly, "perfect Love casts out fear."

The Holy Temple

"Those that be planted in the house of the LORD shall flourish in the courts of our God." I am still and at peace. My heart and my mind are motivated by the spirit of goodness, truth, and beauty. My thought is now on the Presence of God within me; this stills my mind.

I know that the way of creation is Spirit moving upon its self. My True Self now moves in and on itself creating peace, harmony, and health in my body and affairs. I am Divine in my deeper self. I know I am a son of the living God; I create the way God creates by the self-contemplation of spirit. I know my body does not move of itself. It is acted upon by my thoughts and emotions.

I now say to my body, "Be still and quiet." It must obey. I understand this and I know it is a Divine Law. I take my attention away from the physical world; I feast in the House of God within me. I meditate and feast upon harmony, health, and peace; these come forth from the God-Essence within; I am at peace. My body is a temple of the Living God. God is in His Holy Temple; let all the earth keep silent before Him.

ACCEPT ABUNDANCE

- God is the Eternal Now
- The Way of Prayer
- How to Realize the Abundant Life
- The Prayer of Faith
- The Abundant Life
- Imagination, the Workshop of God
- God's Will For Me
- Abide in the Silence
- To Be, To Do, and To Have

God is the Eternal Now
(Using the Subconscious Mind)

Know that my good is this very moment. I believe in my heart that I can prophesy for myself harmony, health, peace, and joy. I enthrone the concept of peace, success, and prosperity in my mind now. I know and believe these thoughts (seeds) will grow and manifest themselves in my experience.

I am the gardener; as I sow, so shall I reap. I sow God-like thoughts (seeds); these wonderful seeds are peace, success, harmony, and goodwill. It is a wonderful harvest.

From this moment forward I am depositing in the Universal Bank (my subconscious mind) seeds or thoughts of peace, confidence, poise, and balance. I am drawing out the fruit of the wonderful seeds I am depositing. I believe and accept the fact that my desire is a seed deposited in the subconscious. I make it real by feeling the reality of it. I accept the reality of my desire in the same manner I accept the fact that the seed deposited in the ground will grow. I know it grows in the darkness; also, my desire or ideal grows in the darkness of my subconscious mind; in a little while, like the seed, it comes above the ground (becomes objectified) as a condition, circumstance, or event.

Infinite Intelligence governs and guides me in all ways. I meditate on whatsoever things are true, honest, just, lovely, and of good report. I think on these things, and God's Power is with my thoughts of Good. I am at peace.

The Way of Prayer

"Thou shall make thy way prosperous, and then thou shall have good success." I now give a pattern of success and prosperity to the deep mind within me, which is the law. I now identify myself with the Infinite Source of supply. I listen to the still, small voice of God within me. This inner voice leads, guides, and governs all of my activities. I am one with the abundance of God. I know and believe that there are new and better ways of conducting my business; Infinite Intelligence reveals the new ways to me.

I am growing in wisdom and understanding. My business is God's business. I am divinely prospered in all ways. Divine Wisdom within me reveals the ways and means by which all of my affairs are adjusted in the right way immediately.

The words of faith and conviction which I now speak open up all the necessary doors or avenues for my success and prosperity. I know that "The Lord (Law) will perfect that which concerns me." My feet are kept in the perfect path, because I am a son of the living God.

How to Realize the Abundant Life

I know that *to prosper* means to grow spiritually along all lines. God is prospering me now in mind, body, and affairs. God's ideas constantly unfold within me bringing to me health, wealth, and perfect Divine expression.

I thrill inwardly as I feel the Life of God vitalizing every atom of my being. I know that God's Life is animating, sustaining, and strengthening me now. I am now expressing a perfect, radiant body full of vitality, energy, and power.

My business or profession is a Divine activity, and since it is God's business, it is successful and prosperous. I imagine and feel an inner wholeness functioning through my body, mind, and affairs. I give thanks, and rejoice in the abundant life.

The Prayer of Faith

"The prayer of faith shall save the sick man, and God shall raise him up." I know that no matter what the negation of yesterday was, that my prayer or affirmation of truth will rise triumphantly over it today. I steadfastly behold the joy of the answered prayer. I walk all day long in the Light.

Today is God's day; it is a glorious day for me, as it is full of peace, harmony, and joy. My faith in the good is written in my heart and felt in my inward parts. I am absolutely convinced that there is a Presence and a perfect Law which receives the impress of my desire now, and which irresistibly attracts into my experience all the good things my heart desires. I now place all of my reliance, faith, and trust in the Power and Presence of God within me; I am at peace.

I know I am a guest of the Infinite, and that God is my Host. I hear the invitation of the Holy One saying, "Come unto me all ye that labor, and I will give you rest." I rest in God; all is well.

The Abundant Life

"Consider the Lilies of the field; they toil not, neither do they spin; yet Solomon in all of his glory was not arrayed as one of these." I know that God is prospering me in all ways. I am now leading the abundant life, because I believe in a God of abundance. I am supplied with everything that contributes to my beauty, well-being, progress, and peace. I am daily experiencing the fruits of the spirit of God within me; I accept my good now; I walk in the light that all good is mine. I am peaceful, poised, serene, and calm. I am one with the source of life; all of my needs are met at every moment of time and every point of space. I now bring "all the empty vessels" to the Father within. The fullness of God is made manifest in all of the departments of my life. "All that the Father hath is mine." I rejoice that this is so.

Imagination, the Workshop of God

"Where there is no vision, the people perish." My vision is that I desire to know more of God, and the way He works. My vision is for perfect health, harmony, and peace. My vision is the inner faith that Infinite Spirit heals and guides me now in all ways. I know and believe that the God-Power within me answers my prayer; this is a deep conviction within me.

I know that imagination is the result of what I image in my mind. "Faith is," as Paul says, "the substance out of which the image is formed."

I make it my daily practice to imagine only for myself and others that which is noble, wonderful, and Christ-like. I now imagine that I am doing the thing I long to do; I imagine that I now possess the things I long to possess; I imagine I am what I long to be. To make it real, I feel the reality of it; I know that it is so. Thank you, Father.

God's Will For Me

"God opens for me the windows of heaven, and pours me out a blessing."

God's will must be God-like; for that is the nature of God. God's will for me, therefore, is health, goodness, harmony, and abundance.

"If ye abide in me, and my words abide in you, ye shall ask what ye will, and it shall be done unto you." I am now enlightened by the truth; each day I am growing in wisdom and understanding. I am a perfect channel for the works of God; I am free from all worry and confusion. Infinite Intelligence within me is a lamp unto my feet. I know I am led to do the right thing; for it is God in action in all of my affairs.

The peace that passes understanding fills my mind now. I believe and accept my ideal. I know it subsists in the Infinite. I give it form and expression by my complete mental acceptance. I feel the reality of the fulfilled desire. The peace of God fills my soul.

Abide in the Silence

Jesus said, "God is a Spirit: and they that worship him must worship him in spirit and in truth." I know and realize that God is a spirit moving within me. I know that God is a feeling or deep conviction of harmony, health, and peace within me; it is the movement of my own heart. The spirit or feeling of confidence and faith which now possesses me is the spirit of God and the action of God on the waters of my mind; this is God; it is the creative Power within me. I live, move, and have my being in the faith and confidence that goodness, truth, and beauty shall follow me all of the days of my life; this faith in God and all things good is omnipotent; it removes all barriers. I now close the door of the senses; I withdraw all attention from the world. I turn within to the One, the Beautiful, and the Good; here, I dwell with my Father beyond time and space; here, I live, move, and dwell in the shadow of the Almighty. I am free from all fear, from the verdict of the world, and the appearance of things. I now feel His Presence which is the feeling of the answered prayer, or the presence of my good. I become that which I contemplate. I now feel that I am what I want to be; this feeling or awareness is the action of God in me; it is the creative Power. I give thanks for the joy of the answered prayer, and I rest in the silence that "It is done."

To Be, To Do, and To Have

At the center of my being is Peace; this is the peace of God. In this stillness I feel strength, guidance, and the Love of His Holy Presence. I am divinely active; I am expressing the fullness of God along all lines. I am a channel for the Divine, and I now release the imprisoned splendor that is within. I am divinely guided to my true expression in life; I am compensated in a wonderful way. I see God in everything and personified in all men everywhere. I know as I permit this river of peace to flow through my being, all of my problems are solved. All things I need to fully express myself on this plane are irresistibly attracted to me by the Universal Law of attraction. The way is revealed to me; I am full of joy and harmony.

Love, Personality, Human, and Family Relationships

- God's Broadcast
- Spiritual Rebirth
- Love Frees
- The Secret Place
- Control Your Emotions
- Prayer of Gratitude
- How to Attract Your Divine Companion
- How to Pray for Companionship
- Divine Freedom
- Prayer for Peace

God's Broadcast

"All ye are brethren, for one is your father."

I always bring harmony, peace, and joy into every situation and into all of my personal relationships. I know, believe, and claim that the peace of God reigns supreme in the mind and heart of everyone in my home and business. No matter what the problem is, I always maintain peace, poise, patience, and wisdom. I fully and freely forgive everyone, regardless of what they may have said or done. I cast all of my burdens on the Christ within; I go free; this is a marvelous feeling. I know that blessings come to me as I forgive.

I see the angel of God's Presence behind every problem or

difficult situation. I know the solution is there, and that everything is working out in Divine order. I trust the God-Presence implicitly; it has the *know-how* of accomplishment. The Absolute Order of Heaven and His Absolute Wisdom are acting through me now and at all times; I know that order is Heaven's first law. My mind is now fixed joyously and expectantly on this perfect harmony. I know the result is the inevitable, perfect solution; my answer is God's answer; it is Divine; for it is the melody of God's broadcast.

Spiritual Rebirth

Today I am reborn spiritually! I completely detach myself from the old way of thinking, and I bring Divine love, light, and truth definitely into my experience. I consciously feel love for everyone I meet. Mentally I say to everyone I contact, "I see the Christ in you, and I know you see the Christ in me." I recognize the qualities of God in everyone. I practice this morning, noon, and night; it is a living part of me.

I am reborn spiritually now, because all day long I practice the Presence of God. No matter what I am doing—whether I am walking the street, shopping, or about my daily business—whenever my thought wanders away from God or the good, I bring it back to the contemplation of His Holy Presence. I feel noble, dignified, and Christ-like. I walk in a high mood sensing my oneness with God. His peace fills my soul.

Love Frees

God is Love, and God is Life; this Life is one and indivisible. Life manifests itself in and through all people; it is at the center of my own being.

I know that light dispels the darkness, so does the love of the good overcome all evil. My knowledge of the power of Love overcomes all negative conditions now. Love and hate cannot dwell together. I now turn the Light of God upon all fear or anxious thoughts in my mind, and they flee away. The dawn (light of truth) appears and the shadows (fear and doubt) flee away.

I know Divine Love watches over me, guides me, and makes clear the path for me. I am expanding into the Divine. I am now expressing God in all of my thoughts, words, and actions; the nature of God is Love. I know that "perfect Love casteth out fear."

The Secret Place

"He that dwelled in the secret place of the most high shall abide under the shadow of the Almighty."

I dwell in the secret place of the most high; this is my own mind. All of my thoughts entertained by me conform to harmony, peace, and goodwill. My mind is the dwelling place of happiness, joy, and a deep sense of security. All of the thoughts that enter my mind contribute to my joy, peace, and general welfare. I live, move, and have my being in the atmosphere of good fellowship, love, and unity.

All of the people that dwell in my mind are God's children. I am at peace in my mind with all of the members of my household and all mankind. The same good I wish for myself, I wish for all men. I am living in the house of God now. I claim peace and happiness, for I know I dwell in the house of the Lord forever.

Control Your Emotions

"*He that is* slow to wrath is of great understanding: but *he that is* hasty of spirit exalteth folly." I am always poised, serene, and calm. The peace of God floods my mind and my whole being. I practice the Golden Rule and sincerely wish peace and goodwill to all men.

I know that the love of all things which are good penetrates my mind casting out all fear. I am now living in the joyous expectancy of the best. My mind is free from all worry and doubt. My words of truth now dissolve every negative thought and emotion within me. I forgive everyone; I open the doorway of my heart to God's Presence. My whole being is flooded with the light and understanding from within.

The petty things of life no longer irritate me. When fear, worry, and doubt knock at my door, faith in goodness, truth, and beauty opens the door, and there is no one there. O God, thou art my God, and there is none else.

Prayer of Gratitude

"O give thanks unto the Lord; call upon His name; make known His deeds among the people. Sing unto him, sing psalms unto him: talk ye of all his wondrous works. Glory ye in His holy name: let the heart of them rejoice that seek the Lord."

I give thanks sincerely .and humbly for all of the goodness, truth, and beauty which flow through me. I have a grateful, uplifted heart for all of the good that has come to me in mind, body, and affairs. I radiate love and goodwill to all mankind. I lift them up in my thought and feeling. I always show my gratitude, and give thanks for all of my blessings. The grateful heart brings my mind and heart in intimate union with the creative Power of the Cosmos. My thankful and exalted state of mind leads me along the ways by which all good things come. "Enter into his gates with thanksgiving, and into his courts with praise: Be thankful unto him, and bless his name."

How to Attract Your Divine Companion

I know that I am one with God now. In Him I live, move, and have my being. God is Life; this life is the life of all men and women. We are all sons and daughters of the one Father.

I know and believe there is a man waiting to love and cherish me. I know I can contribute to his happiness and peace. He loves my ideals, and I love his ideals. He does not want to make me over; neither do I want to make him over. There is mutual love, freedom, and respect.

There is one mind; I know him now in this mind. I unite now with the qualities and attributes that I admire and want expressed by my husband. I am one with them in my mind. We know and love each other already in Divine Mind. I see the Christ in him; he sees the Christ in me. Having met him *within, I* must meet him in the *without;* for this is the law of my own mind.

These words go forth and accomplish whereunto they are sent. I know it is now done, finished, and accomplished in God. Thank you, Father.

How to Pray for Companionship

God is one and indivisible. In Him we love, move, and have our being. I know and believe that God indwells every person; I am one with God and with all people. I now attract the right person who is in complete accord with me. This is a spiritual union, because it is the spirit of God functioning through the personality of someone with whom I blend perfectly. I know I can give to this person love, light, and truth. I know I can make this man's life full, complete, and wonderful.

I now decree that he possesses the following qualities and attributes; i.e., he is spiritual, loyal, faithful, and true. He is prosperous, peaceful, and happy. We are irresistibly attracted to each other. Only that which belongs to love, truth, and wholeness can enter my experience. I accept my ideal companion now.

Divine Freedom

"If ye continue in my word, then are ye my disciples indeed: And ye shall know the truth, and the truth shall make you free." I know the truth, and the truth is that the realization of my desire would free me from all sense of bondage. I accept my freedom; I know it is already established in the Kingdom of God.

I know that all things in my world are projections of my inner attitudes. I am transforming my mind by dwelling on whatsoever things are true, lovely, noble, and Christ-like. I contemplate myself now as possessing all of the good things of Life, such as peace, harmony, health, and happiness.

My contemplation rises to the point of acceptance; I accept the desires of my heart completely. God is the only presence. I am expressing the fullness of God now. I am free! There is peace in my home, heart, and in all of my affairs.

Prayer for Peace

Peace begins with me. The peace of God fills my mind; the spirit of goodwill goes forth from me to all mankind. God is everywhere, and fills the hearts of all men. In absolute truth all men are now spiritually perfect; they are expressing God's qualities and attributes. These qualities and attributes are Love, Light, Truth, and Beauty.

There are no separate nations. All men belong to the One Country—the One Nation which is God's Country. A country is a dwelling place; I dwell in the secret place of the Most High; I walk and talk with God; so do all men everywhere. There is only One Divine Family, and that is humanity.

There are no frontiers or barriers between nations, because God is One; God is indivisible. God cannot be divided against Himself. The love of God permeates the hearts of all men everywhere. God and His Wisdom rules and guides the nation; He inspires our leaders and the leaders of all nations to do His will, and His will only. The peace of God which passes all understanding fills my mind and the minds of all men throughout the cosmos. Thank you, Father, for Thy peace; it is done.

EXPRESSION

- Predicting My Future
- My Destiny
- Constructive Imagination
- The Balanced Mind
- The Creative Word
- The Answered Prayer
- The Divine Answer
- Divine Guidance
- Right Action
- The Resurrection of My Desire
- Achieving My Goal
- Business Problems
- Principle in Business
- How to Solve Your Problems
- Steps To Success
- The Triumph of Prayer

Predicting My Future

"Thou madest him to have dominion over the works of thy hands." I know that my faith in God determines my future. My faith in God means my faith in all things good. I unite myself now with true ideas, and I know the future will be in the image and likeness of my habitual thinking. "As a man thinketh in his heart so is he."

From this moment forward my thoughts are on: "Whatsoever things are true, whatsoever things are honest, whatsoever things are just, whatsoever things are lovely, and of good report;" day and night I meditate on these things, and I know these seeds (thoughts) which I habitually dwell upon will become a rich harvest for me. I am the captain of my own soul; I am the master of my fate; for my thought and feeling are my destiny.

My Destiny

I know that I mold, fashion, and create my own destiny. My faith in God is my destiny; this means an abiding faith in all things good. I live in the joy-out expectancy of the best; only the best comes to me. I know the harvest I will reap in the future, because all of my thoughts are God's thoughts, and God is with my thoughts of good. My thoughts are the seeds of goodness, truth, and beauty. I now place my thoughts of love, peace, joy, success, and goodwill in the garden of my mind. This is God's garden, and it will yield an abundant harvest. The glory and beauty of God will be expressed in my life. From this moment forward, I express life, love, and truth. I am radiantly happy and prosperous in all ways. Thank you, Father.

Constructive Imagination

"Those things, which ye have both learned, and received, and heard, and seen in me, do: and the God of peace shall be with you."

My mind is God's Mind, and my thoughts are God's thoughts. This is how I use my imagination daily: I constantly meditate on whatsoever things are true, honest, just, lovely, and of good report; my imagination is the workshop of God at all times. I imagine only peace, harmony, health, wealth, perfect expression, and love. I reject everything unlike God or perfection.

Today I claim my true place in the Kingdom of God. I make it a daily practice to seek first the Kingdom of God within me; then I know that all good things shall be added to me. All of my faith is in God and the good. God's Love is supreme in me, and casts out all fear. I am at peace. I thank you, Father.

The Balanced Mind

"Thou wilt keep him in perfect peace whose mind is stayed on thee, because he trusted in thee." I know that the inner desires of my heart come from God within me. God wants me to be happy. The will of God for me is life, love, truth, and beauty. I mentally accept my good now, and I become a perfect, free, flowing channel for the Divine.

I come into His Presence singing; I enter into His courts with praise; I am joyful and happy; I am still and poised.

The Still Small Voice whispers in my ear revealing to me my perfect answer. I am an expression of God. I am always in my true place doing the thing I love to do. I refuse to accept the opinions of man as truth. I now turn within, and I sense and feel the rhythm of the Divine. I hear the melody of God whispering its message of love to me.

My mind is God's mind, and I am always reflecting Divine wisdom and Divine intelligence. My brain symbolizes the Christ capacity to think wisely and spiritually. God's ideas unfold within my mind with perfect sequence. I am always poised, balanced, serene, and calm; for I know that God will always reveal to me the perfect solution to all of my needs.

The Creative Word

"Be ye doers of the word, and not hearers only, deceiving your own selves." My creative word is my silent conviction that my prayer is answered. When I speak the word for healing, success, or prosperity, my word is spoken in the consciousness of Life and Power, knowing that it is done. My word has power, because it is one with Omnipotence. The words I speak are always constructive and creative. When I pray, my words are full of life, love, and feeling; this makes my affirmations, thoughts, and words creative. I know the greater my faith behind the word spoken, the more power it has. The words I use form a definite mold, which determine what form my thought is to take. Divine Intelligence operates through me now, and reveals to me what I need to know. I have the answer now. I am at peace. God is Peace.

The Answered Prayer

"Before they call, I will answer; and while they are yet speaking, I will hear."

When I pray, I call on the Father, the Son, and the Holy Ghost; the Father is my own consciousness; the Son is my desire; the Holy Ghost is the feeling of being what I want to be.

I now take my attention away from the problem, whatever it may be. My mind and heart are open to the influx from on High.

I know the Kingdom of God is within me. I sense, feel, understand, and know that my own life, my awareness of being, my own I am-ness, is the Living Spirit Almighty. I now turn in recognition to this One Who Forever Is; the Light of God illumines my pathway; I am Divinely inspired and governed in all ways.

Now I begin to pray scientifically in order to bring my desire into manifestation by claiming and feeling myself to be and to have what I long to be and to have. I walk in the inner silent knowing of the soul, because I know my prayer is already answered, as I feel the reality of it in my heart. Thank you, Father; it is done!

The Divine Answer

I know that the answer to my problem lies in the God-Self within me. I now get quiet, still, and relaxed. I am at peace. I know God speaks in peace and not in confusion. I am now in tune with the Infinite; I know and believe implicitly that Infinite Intelligence is revealing to me the perfect answer. I think about the solution to my problems. I now live in the mood I would have were my problem solved. I truly live in this abiding faith and trust which is the mood of the solution; this is the spirit of God moving within me. This Spirit is Omnipotent; it is manifesting itself; my whole being rejoices in the solution; I am glad. I live in this feeling, and give thanks.

I know that God has the answer. With God all things are possible. God is the Living Spirit Almighty within me; He is the source of all wisdom and illumination.

The indicator of the Presence of God within me is a sense of peace and poise. I now cease all sense of strain and struggle; I trust the God-Power implicitly. I know that all the Wisdom and Power I need to live a glorious and successful life are within me. I relax my entire body; I cast all burdens on the Christ; I go free. I claim and feel the Peace of God flooding my mind, heart, and whole being. I know the quiet mind gets its problems solved. I now turn the request over to the God-Presence knowing It has an answer. I am at peace.

Divine Guidance

I now dwell on the Omnipresence and Omni action of God. I know that this Infinite Wisdom guides the planets on their source. I know this same Divine Intelligence governs and directs all of my affairs. I claim and believe Divine understanding is mine at all times. I know that all of my activities are controlled by this indwelling Presence. All of my motives are God-like and true.

177

God's wisdom, truth, and beauty are being expressed by me at all times. The All-Knowing One within me knows what to do, and how to do it. My business or profession is completely controlled, governed, and directed by the love of God. Divine guidance is mine. I know God's answer, for my mind is at peace. I rest in the Everlasting Arms.

Right Action

I radiate goodwill to all mankind in thought, word, and deed. I know the peace and goodwill that I radiate to my fellowman come back to me a thousand fold. Whatever I need to know comes to me from the God-Self within me. Infinite Intelligence is operating through me revealing to me what I need to know. God in me knows only the answer. The perfect answer is made known to me now. Infinite Intelligence and Divine Wisdom make all decisions through me, and there is only right action and right expression taking place in my life. Every night I wrap myself in the Mantle of God's Love, and fall asleep knowing Divine Guidance is mine. When the dawn comes, I am filled with peace. I go forth into the new day full of faith, confidence, and trust. Thank you, Father.

The Resurrection of My Desire

My desire for health, harmony, peace, abundance, and security is the voice of God speaking to me. I definitely choose to be happy and successful. I am guided in all ways. I open my mind and heart to the influx of the Holy Spirit; I am at peace. I draw successful and happy people into my experience. I recognize only the Presence and Power of God within me.

The Light of God shines through me and from me into everything about me. The emanation of God's Love flows from me; it is a healing radiance unto everyone who comes into my Presence.

I now assume the feeling of being what I want to be. I know that the way to resurrect my desire is to remain faithful to my ideal, knowing that an Almighty Power is working in my behalf. I live in this mood of faith and confidence; I give thanks that it is done; for it is established in God, and all is well.

Achieving My Goal

"In all thy ways acknowledge Him, and He will make plain thy path." My knowledge of God and the way He works is growing by leaps and bounds. I control and direct all of my emotions along peaceful, constructive channels. Divine Love fills all of my thoughts, words, and actions. My mind is at peace; I am at peace with my fellowman. I am always relaxed and at ease. I know that I am here to express God fully in all ways. I believe implicitly in the guidance of the Holy Spirit within. This Infinite Intelligence within me now reveals to me the perfect plan of expression; I move toward it confidently and joyously. The goal and the objective that I have in my mind is good and very good. I have definitely planted in my mind the way of fulfillment. The Almighty Power now moves in my behalf; He is a Light on my path.

Business Problems

I know and believe my business is God's business; God is my partner in all of my affairs; to me this means His light, love, truth, and inspiration fill my mind and heart in all ways. I solve all of my problems by placing my complete trust in the Divine Power within me. I know that this Presence sustains everything. I now rest in security and peace. This day I am surrounded by perfect understanding; there is a Divine solution to all of my problems. I definitely understand everyone; I am understood. I know that all of my business relationships are in accord with the Divine Law of Harmony. I know that Christ indwells all of my customers and clients. I work harmoniously with others to the end that happiness, prosperity, and peace reign supreme.

Principle in Business

My business is God's business. I am always about my Father's business which is to radiate Life, Love, and Truth to all mankind. I am expressing myself fully now; I am giving of my talents in a wonderful way. I am Divinely compensated.

God is prospering my business, profession, or activity in a wonderful way. I claim that all of those in my organization are spiritual links in its growth, welfare, and prosperity; I know this, believe it, and rejoice that it is so. All of those connected with me are Divinely prospered and illumined by the Light.

The Light that lighteth every man that cometh into the world leads and guides me in all ways. All of my decisions are controlled by Divine Wisdom. Infinite Intelligence reveals better ways in which I can serve humanity. I rest in the Lord forever.

How to Solve Your Problems

"What things so ever you desire, when you pray, believe that ye receive them, and ye shall have them." I know that a problem has its solution within it in the form of a desire. The realization of my desire is good and very good. I know and believe that the creative Power within me has the absolute Power to bring forth that which I deeply desire. The Principle which gave me the desire is the Principle which gives it birth. There is absolutely no argument in my mind about this.

I now ride the white horse which is the spirit of God moving upon the waters of my mind. I take my attention away from the problem, and dwell upon the reality of the fulfilled desire. I am using the Law now. I assume the feeling that my prayer is answered. I make it real by feeling the reality of it. In Him I live, move, and have my being; I live in this feeling, and give thanks.

Steps To Success

"Would you not that I be about my Father's business." I know that my business, profession, or activity is God's business. God's business is always basically successful. I am growing in wisdom and understanding every day. I know, believe, and accept the fact that God's law of abundance is always working for me, through me, and all around me.

My business or profession is full of right action and right expression. The ideas, money, merchandise, and contacts that I need are mine now and at all times. All of these things are irresistibly attracted to me by the law of universal attraction. God is the life of my business; I am Divinely guided and inspired in all ways. Every day I am presented with wonderful opportunities to grow, expand, and progress. I am building up goodwill. I am a great success, because I do business with others, as I would have them do it with me.

The Triumph of Prayer

I now let go of everything; I enter into the realization of peace, harmony, and joy. God is all, over all, through all, and all in all. I lead the triumphant life, because I know that Divine Love guides, directs, sustains, and heals me. The immaculate Presence of God is at the very center of my being; it is made manifest now in every atom of my body. There can be no delay, impediment, or obstructions to the realization of my heart's desire. The Almighty

Power of God is now moving in my behalf. "None shall stay its hand, and say unto it, 'what doest thou?'" I know what I want; my desire is clear-cut and definite. I accept it completely in my mind. I remain faithful to the end. I have entered into Jerusalem; this means my mind is at peace.

About the Author

Dr. Joseph Murphy was born on May 20, 1898, in a small town in the County of Cork, Ireland. His father, Denis Murphy, was a deacon and professor at the National School of Ireland, a Jesuit facility. His mother, Ellen, née Connelly, was a housewife, who later gave birth to another son, John, and a daughter, Catherine.

Joseph was brought up in a strict Catholic household. His father was quite devout and, indeed, was one of the few lay professors who taught Jesuit seminarians. He had a broad knowledge of many subjects and developed in his son the desire to study and learn.

Ireland at that time was suffering from one of its many economic depressions, and many families were starving. Although Denis Murphy was steadily employed, his income was barely enough to sustain the family.

Young Joseph was enrolled in the National School and was a brilliant student. He was encouraged to study for the priesthood and was accepted as a Jesuit seminarian. However, by the time he reached his late teen years, he began to question the Catholic orthodoxy of the Jesuits, and he withdrew from the seminary. Since his goal was to explore new ideas and gain new experiences—a goal he could not pursue in Catholic-dominated Ireland—he left his family to go to America.

He arrived at the Ellis Island Immigration Center with only $5 in his pocket. His first project was to find a place to live. He was fortunate to locate a rooming house where he shared a room with a pharmacist who worked in local drugstore.

Joseph's knowledge of English was minimal, as Gaelic was spoken both in his home and at school, so like most Irish immigrants, Joseph worked as a day laborer, earning enough to keep fed and housed.

He and his roommate became good friends, and when a job opened up at the drugstore where his friend worked, he was hired to be an assistant to the pharmacist. He immediately enrolled in a school to study pharmacy. With his keen mind and desire to learn, it didn't take long before Joseph passed the qualification exams and became a full-fledged pharmacist. He now made enough money to rent his own apartment. After a few years, he purchased the drugstore, and for the next few years ran a successful business.

When the United States entered World War II, Joseph enlisted in the Army and was assigned to work as a pharmacist in the medical unit of the 88th Infantry Division. At that time, he renewed his interest in religion and began to read extensively about various religious beliefs. After his discharge from the Army, he chose not to return to his career in pharmacy. He traveled extensively, taking courses in several universities both in the United States and abroad.

From his studies, Joseph became enraptured by the various Asian religions and went to India to learn about them in depth. He studied all of the major religions from the time of their beginning. He extended these studies to the great philosophers from ancient times until the present.

Although he studied with some of the most intelligent and far-sighted professors, the one person who most influenced Joseph was Dr. Thomas Troward, who was a judge as well as a philosopher, doctor, and professor. Judge Troward became Joseph's mentor. From him he not only learned philosophy, theology, and law, but also was introduced to mysticism and particularly, the Masonic order. He became an active member of this order and over the years rose in the Masonic ranks to the 32nd degree in the Scottish Rite.

Upon his return to the United States, Joseph chose to become a minister and bring his broad knowledge to the public. As his concept of Christianity was not traditional and indeed ran counter to most of the Christian denominations, he founded his own church in Los Angeles. He attracted a small number of congregants, but it did not take long for his message of optimism and hope rather than the "sin and damnation" sermons of so many ministers to attract many men and women to his church.

Dr. Joseph Murphy was a proponent of the New Thought movement. This movement was developed in the late 19th and early 20th centuries by many philosophers and deep thinkers who studied this phenomenon and preached, wrote, and practiced a new way of looking at life. By combining a metaphysical, spiritual, and pragmatic approach to the way we think and live, they uncovered the secret of attaining what we truly desire.

The proponents of the New Thought movement preached a new idea of life that brings out new methods and more perfected results, and we have the power to use it to enrich our lives. We can do all these things only as we have found the law and worked out the understanding of the law, which God seemed to have written in riddles in the past.

Of course, Dr. Murphy wasn't the only minister to preach this positive message. Several churches, whose ministers and congregants were influenced by the New Thought movement, were founded and developed in the decades following World War II. The Church of Religious Science, the Unity Church, and similar places of worship preach philosophies similar to this. Dr. Murphy named his organization The Church of Divine Science. He often shared platforms, conducted joint programs with his similar-thinking colleagues, and trained other men and women to join their ministry.

Over the years, other churches joined with him in developing an organization called the Federation of Divine Science, which acts an umbrella for all Divine Science churches. Each of the Divine Science church leaders continues to push for more education, and Dr. Murphy was one of the leaders to support the creation of the Divine Science School in St. Louis, Missouri, to train new ministers and provide ongoing educational education for both ministers and congregants.

The annual meeting of the Divine Science ministers was a must to attend, and Dr. Murphy was a featured speaker at them. He encouraged the participants to study and continue to learn, particularly about the importance of the subconscious mind.

Over the next few years, Murphy's local Church of Divine Science grew so large that his building was too small to hold them. He rented The Wilshire Ebell Theater, a former movie theater. His services were so well attended that even this venue could not always accommodate all who wished to attend. Classes conducted by Dr. Murphy and his staff supplemented his Sunday services that were attended by 1,300 to 1,500 people. These were supplemented by seminars and lectures that were held most days and evenings. The church remained at the Wilshire Ebell Theater in Los Angeles until 1976, when it moved to a new location in Laguna Hills, California, near a retirement community.

To reach the vast numbers of people who wanted to hear his message, Dr. Murphy created a weekly radio talk show, which eventually reached an audience of over a million listeners.

Many of his followers wanted more than just summaries and suggested that he tape his lectures and radio programs. He was at first reluctant to do so, but agreed to experiment. His radio programs were recorded on extra-large 78 rpm discs, a common practice at that time. He had six cassettes made from one of these discs and placed them on the information table in the lobby of the Wilshire Ebell Theater. They sold out the first hour. This started a new venture. His tapes of his lecture explaining biblical texts, and providing meditations and prayers for his listeners were not only sold in his church, but in other churches, bookstores, and via the mail.

As the church grew, Dr. Murphy added a staff of professional and administrative personnel to assist him in the many programs in which he was involved and in researching and preparing his first books. One of the most effective members of his staff was his administrative secretary, Dr. Jean Wright. The working relationship developed into a romance, and they were married—a lifelong partnership that enriched both of their lives.

At this time (the 1950s), there were very few major publishers of spiritually inspired material. The Murphy's located some small publishers in the Los Angeles area, and with them produced a series of small books (often 30 to 50 pages printed in pamphlet form) that were sold, mostly in churches, from $1.50 to $3.00 per book. When the orders for these books increased to the point where they required second and third printings, major publishers recognized that there was a market for such books and added them to their catalogs.

Dr. Murphy became well known outside of the Los Angeles area as a result of his books, tapes, and radio broadcasts and was invited to lecture all over the country. He did not limit his lectures to religious matters, but spoke on the historical values of life, the art of wholesome living, and on the teachings of great philosophers—both from the Western and Oriental cultures.

As Dr. Murphy never learned to drive, he had to arrange for somebody to drive him to the various places where he was invited to lecture and other places in his very busy schedule. One of Jean's functions as his administrative secretary and later as his wife was to plan his assignments, arrange for trains or flights, airport pickups, hotel accommodations, and all the other details of the trips.

The Murphy's traveled frequently to many countries around the world. One of his favorite working vacations was to hold seminars on cruise ships. These trips were for a week or more and would take him to many countries around the world.

One of Dr. Murphy's most rewarding activities was speaking to the inmates at many prisons. Many ex-convicts wrote him over the years, telling him how his words had truly turned their lives around and inspired them to live spiritual and meaningful lives.

He toured the United States and many countries in Europe and Asia. In his lectures, he emphasized the importance of understanding the power of the subconscious mind and the life principles based on belief in the one God, the "I AM."

Dr. Murphy's pamphlet-sized books were so popular that he began to expand them into more detailed and longer works. His wife gave us some insight into his manner and method of writing. She reported that he wrote his manuscripts on a tablet and pressed so hard on his pencil or pen that you could read the page by the imprint on the next page. He seemed to be in a trance while writing. His writing style was to remain in his office for four to six hours without disturbance until he stopped and said that was enough for the day. Each day was the same. He never went back into the office again until the next morning to finish what he'd started. He took no food or drink while he was working, He was just alone with his thoughts and his huge library of books, to which he referred from time to time. His wife sheltered him from visitors and calls and kept things moving for church business and other activities.

Dr. Murphy was always looking for a simple way to discuss the issues and to elaborate points that would explain in detail how it affects the individual. He chose some of his lectures to present on cassettes, records, or CDs, as the technologies developed and new methods entered the audio field.

His entire work of CDs and cassettes are tools that can be used for most problems that individuals encounter in life, and have been time-tested to accomplish the goals as intended. His basic theme is that the solution to problems lies within oneself. Outside elements cannot change one's thinking. That is, your mind is your own. To live a better life, it's your mind not outside circumstances that you must change. You create your own destiny. The power of change is in your mind, and by using the power of your subconscious mind, you can make those changes for the better.

Dr. Murphy wrote more than 30 books. His most famous work, *The Power of the Unconscious Mind*, which was first published in 1963, became an immediate bestseller. It was acclaimed as one of the best self-help guides ever written. Millions of copies have been sold and continue to be sold all over the world.

Among some of his other best-selling books were *Telepsychics—The Magic Power of Perfect Living, The Amazing Laws of Cosmic Mind, Secrets of the I-Ching, The Miracle of Mind Dynamics, Your Infinite Power to Be Rich,* and *The Cosmic Power Within You.*

Dr. Murphy died in December 1981, and his wife, Dr. Jean Murphy, continued his ministry after his death. In a lecture she gave in 1986, quoting her late husband, she reiterated his philosophy:

> I want to teach men and women of their Divine Origin, and the powers regnant within them. I want to inform that this power is within and that they are their own saviors and capable of achieving their own salvation. This is the message of the Bible and nine-tenths of our confusion today is due to wrongful, literal interpretation of the life-transforming truths offered in it.
>
> I want to reach the majority, the man on the street, the woman overburdened with duty and suppression of her talents and abilities. I want to help others at every stage or level of consciousness to learn of the wonders within.

She said of her husband: "He was a practical mystic, possessed by the intellect of a scholar, the mind of a successful executive, the heart of the poet." His message summed up was: "You are the king, the ruler of your world for you are one with God."